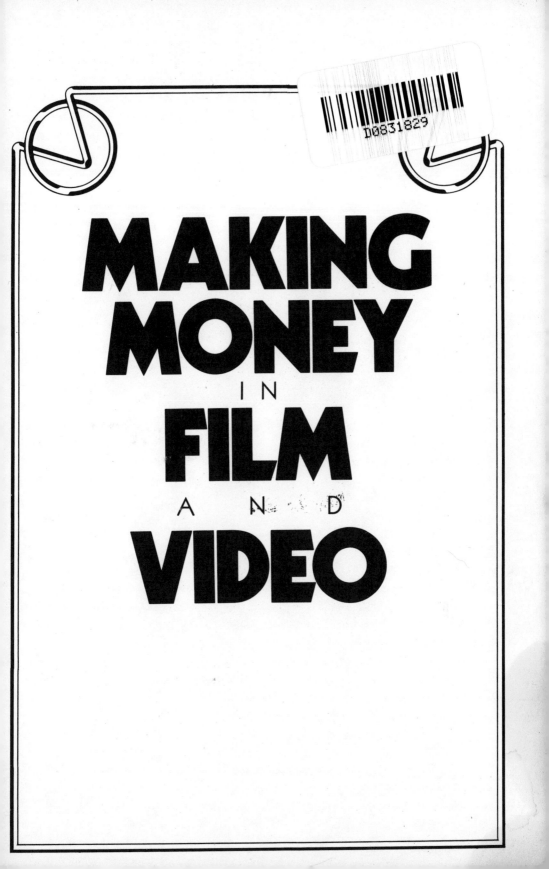

MAKING MONEY

MONEY

IN

FILM

A N D

VIDEO

MAKING MONEY

IN

FILM

AND

VIDEO

A HANDBOOK FOR FREELANCERS AND INDEPENDENTS

RAUL DA SILVA

PRENTICE HALL PRESS • NEW YORK

Copyright © 1986 by Prentice-Hall, Inc.
All rights reserved
including the right of reproduction
in whole or in part in any form

Published by Prentice Hall Press
A Division of Simon & Schuster, Inc.

PRENTICE HALL PRESS is a trademark of Simon & Schuster, In

Library of Congress Cataloging in Publication Data
Da Silva, Raul.
    Making money in film and video.
    Bibliography
    Includes index.
    1. Moving-pictures—Production and direction.
I. Title.
PN1995.9.P7D3   1986   792'.0232'023   84-13065
ISBN 0-671-61411-8

Manufactured in the United States of America

10 9 8 7 6 5 4 3 2 1

Cartoons courtesy of Ray da Silva

To Frank Capra
  what he is
  and what he stands for

ACKNOWLEDGMENTS

This is an experiential handbook and therefore was not a collaborative effort. The only segment written by someone else is the rationale in chapter 6 written by John Hammond, of Rochester, New York. The rationale is extraordinary yet very typical of this wonderful business communicator's work, always above and beyond the call of duty. John Hammond has been a work-ethic role model for many of us.

Through the years, my other role models came into focus, and each in his own quiet way made an indirect contribution to this work by virtue of his own ethics and integrity: Jamison Handy, whose company gave me my first job in films; William Marsteller, whom I nominated for the Advertising Hall of Fame many years ago and who eventually was inducted, I am quite certain in spite of my nomination. To have known and worked for two legends like these in one lifetime leaves one deeply grateful to the powers that be. They more than make up for those who take instead of give to the world.

Then there were others who simply encouraged me through the years. Encouragement is what keeps us going when all else fails. Sal Parlato, who has made major contributions to the film literature through his film reference books, is one of those whose constant faith and trust never faltered through the years. Jack Smith, of the Rochester Institute of Technology, is another. Maxwell Seligman, president of TeleCraft in New York City and a nephew of Joe Brandt, one of the founders of Columbia Pictures, has been wonderful in his support through almost two decades. Jerry Carr and Frank DiProsa, who head commercial television broadcast stations, have uplifted me with their constant faith in my work.

I wish many more women were in the media. The industry is not currently well balanced without women, whose contributions we anticipate.

Two women who must be mentioned here for their contributions to this book are Elizabeth Stege Huttner, an extraordinary editor-organizer, and Barbara Ravage, whose editorial skills and patience helped this book make it to your hands.

CONTENTS

PREFACE

During the 1970s film schools and film departments prolifer-
ated throughout the United States. The core of their curricula
was courses in production techniques and aesthetics. Most
were taught by academicians thoroughly schooled in the the-
ory of filmmaking but generally without practical experience
in the field. As a result, they were unable to provide their
students with insight into the daily task of extracting a liveli-
hood from the film industry.

Film school graduates began to discover that, whereas they
may have been equipped to make a film, they were unquali-
fied to sell their expertise. They had little or no idea where to
take their skills. Who needs film? When? Where? For what
reasons? How much is charged for time? How much, if anything, should they tack on to the purchase price of items
needed to complete a project? These and hundreds of other
questions had to be answered, and they could be answered
only by an experienced filmmaker.

The plight of these students became apparent to me as I interviewed some of them for jobs in my capacity as an executive producer at an advertising agency. Not only did the film students have no training in seeking work, they also had no idea how to write a simple film proposal. They were ignorant of corporate structure and lacked knowledge of advertising, business communications, public relations practices, sales promotion, and the marketing process. Each of these subjects has a practical importance for the working filmmaker.

As a first attempt to address this problem, I wrote a book in 1978 entitled *The Business of Filmmaking*. Although that book explored the intricacies of budgeting and writing proposals, it was a simple introduction to the problem, the tip of the iceberg. Then in 1979 came Mollie Gregory's *Making Films Your Business*, which is a nice expansion on the subject of filmmaking business problems but is not a handbook on survival tactics in screened communications.

The book you hold in your hand is the first of its kind, a thorough exploration of the real world of the filmmaking business. I hope it will go a long way toward answering the many questions you will have as your career unfolds. It will not answer every question, but I guarantee that it will give you the tools necessary to find the answers yourself. On first reading, some of the sections—for example, that on advertising agency personnel—may seem superfluous, but that impression will die quickly once you actually begin to grapple with the daily problems of seeking assignments from advertising shops and large corporations.

The purpose of this book is to build a bridge from the theoretical world of academia to the hard-nosed reality of filmmaking in the practical world. It is not a production or technical manual of any kind. Rather, it presumes certain basic technical knowledge on the part of the reader and therefore uses the terms and phrases of filmmaking vernacular to achieve understanding. The glossary includes the more important of these terms, but it does not provide the extensive and constantly changing vocabulary a production technology book might. It covers instead the terms of selling and marketing that form a basic, unchanging language decades old.

This is a lean, working handbook that should go a long way toward easing you into the business. It is a reference book and has been written to sit on your desk for repeated review until the experience contained within its covers becomes your own. Readers who have already been out in the field may recognize some of the problems described and perhaps have discovered a new solution to them. In some cases it may contain the overlooked piece to an unsolved business puzzle.

Making Money in Film and Video was written to help you survive and succeed in a most competitive business. I have been in it long enough to understand that such competition is good, that your success will also help mine. All of life works that way. We are all interconnected in an enterprise that is both a cause and a way of life. My success is also yours. Go out and make a good film.

PROLOGUE

Max Cleland, who was left with only one arm and no legs by the Vietnam experience, was good enough to send me a poem I heard him read when he took office as the head of the Veterans Administration in the mid-1970s. The poem was written by an unknown Confederate soldier.

Those of you who are midway or beyond in your careers in what must be the cruelest of all possible professions will understand the appropriateness of my now passing on to my readers the poem on the following page.

PRAYER

I asked God for strength, that I might achieve,
I was made weak, that I might learn humbly to
      obey.
I asked for health, that I might do greater things,
I was given infirmity, that I might do better things.
I asked for riches, that I might be happy,
I was given poverty, that I might be wise.
I asked for power, that I might have the praise of
      men,
I was given weakness, that I might feel the need of
      God.
I asked for all things, that I might enjoy life,
I was given life, that I might enjoy all things.
I got nothing that I asked for—but everything I
      had hoped for.
Almost despite myself, my unspoken prayers were
      answered.
I am, among all men, most richly blessed.

1/BEFORE YOU GET STARTED

It was the middle of August and I was sitting straight in my chair to dry the perspiration off my back after walking eight midsummer Manhattan blocks from a mixing studio. The air conditioner was browning out, but I cared little because I was in the company of gods. The place was TeleCraft, over Sardi's, where many great animation spots have been cut. It is not just another editing studio, but one of the world's best, a reputation earned by thirty-five years of quality and reliable work by editors responsible for some of the finest footage to have seen light.

That day a nicely dressed young man came in and looked toward the five of us—all over thirty and representing nearly 125 years' experience in films—sitting clustered in worn director's chairs. He wore a dark suit in the ungodly heat and a wet, white shirt with a grayish tie that looked like it had been loosened and retightened forty times that day. He was, naturally, nervous.

"Er, hi, I . . . was wondering if you could use help, that is, a production assistant, editor, grip, or. . . ." His voice seemed to trail off. We exchanged glances. A visiting producer from Rochester, New York, I declined to answer him. A more outspoken member of our group could not bear seeing the chap suffer anymore. Waving his hand around our circle of experienced filmmakers, he asked, "Do we look like we need any help?"

At a loss for an answer, the kid thanked us and left. I had a helpless tight feeling in my chest. I knew exactly how that young guy felt, even though I had not been in his position for well over fifteen years.

GROUNDWORK

Filmmaking is one of the most difficult industries in the world to break into. It may offer great rewards, both spiritually and financially, but the Hollywood story aside, the real business (and the one that offers the most openings) is film as communication, not entertainment. By communication film I mean educational and training films, audiovisual or presentations pictures, television spots, multimedia for trade shows, and most importantly, videotape, a medium most filmmakers today will be involved with at some point in their careers.

At last count over one thousand schools, colleges, and universities offered some kind of film, video, or audiovisual curriculum. Included in this number are the many small colleges with media departments that endeavor to give students some exposure to nonprint communications. Barely a handful of such programs existed two decades ago. What happened?

The population explosion happened. The need for information happened. The coming of age of boys who fought in wars where the impact of audiovisual propaganda and strategy was felt happened. The time for these seeds to grow and even hybridize happened.

If you are reading this book, it is quite likely that you have completed a media curriculum and are ready to explore the money-making possibilities of film. This is the time to appraise the market and yourself; the early section of this chapter is designed to help you do just that. The second half, which covers advertising agency filmmakers, is offered to assist your self-evaluation. Dreams of an independent film empire aside, you may actually be better suited for agency work. Many independents first apprentice with agencies to acquire experience and something just as valuable—business contacts. At the very least, however, as an independent or freelance filmmaker, you should know how the other half lives.

Where the Action Is

The two largest areas of filmmaking, according to Tom Hope, a consultant who chronicles the audiovisual market each year with his *Hope Reports,* are business and education. These areas offer a broad range of possibilities for the filmmaker. Some, though far from all, are outlined below, beginning in the business realms where audiovisual use is most prevalent.

The public relations offices of major corporations and civic organizations may turn to visuals to enliven corporate shareholders' meetings and annual reports; to present case histories and securities analyses; to enhance internal communications and community relations; or to boost product publicity, perhaps utilizing the corporate puff in a theatrical release.

Filmmaking techniques in advertising and sales promotion are more self-evident. Television commercials, short shorts for nontheatrical distribution, and merchandising films that enhance the product or service, perhaps at point of purchase, enjoy fairly large audiences, while films emphasizing sales presentation, new product demos, and sales training are targeted at smaller audiences.

Multiple uses of film and audiovisual materials can simplify management's workload while providing accurate and attention-grabbing information in personnel fields: technical, management, and skills training; labor relations; orientation; and behavioral education.

Beyond but not excluding the business world, there are also multiple educational markets for film. The medium can increase general awareness of the human condition by probing life values, establishing the need for mutual understanding, or exploring the impact of a larger population and an aging citizenship on the community. Humanity's relationship to its environment is explored in films on conservation, energy, city planning, transportation, and government.

Law enforcement agencies use film for training and informational purposes, while all medical disciplines from physiology and pathology to epidemiology and the study of social drug problems benefit from the filmmaker's ability to capture innovative techniques or historic breakthroughs and transmit them accurately to farflung audiences.

Finally, film can broaden the recreational experience. Ignoring (for the moment) Hollywood entertainment features, film enlarges sports experiences and can teach us basic and even primitive arts.

In each of these areas, filmmakers are turning people away from the inefficiency and lack of immediacy of the print media and toward the sensory impact and practicality that film and other audiovisual media offer.

A Personal Inventory

Now you know the possibilities, but how do they apply to you? Can you answer the following questions without consulting a reference book: What is the function of a securities analyst? What is the function of a securities analyst's meeting and presentation? What exactly is community relations? Can you write a proposal for any of the business fields mentioned above? Can you write an effective budget estimate? Can you actually sell the need for film to a client? Unless you can answer yes to most of these questions, you have limited your scope in filmmaking and your spectrum of operations. You have some homework to do.

Notice that I did not ask you if you can write a script. You can always hire a writer. Or can you? Would you be able to edit a script for accuracy? Would you be able to evaluate it adequately? Or check it prior to presentation to a client to ascertain that all pertinent points are covered?

You say someone else would do that since you are a technician? It takes but a few weeks to learn how to operate a camera, read a light meter, check out the latest emulsions and hardware, read the lab standards book, and learn to operate an editing console or rewind bench. That is all, just a few weeks. I have seen it done; I have taken writers in hand and made producers out of them in a few weeks. But make writers out of producers? It cannot be done in a few weeks, seldom in months, and often not even in years.

Putting the writing aside, where do you fit if you lack a business background? Ask yourself if you could possibly help a producer who needs someone to produce and direct from hard script. Can you do that with the education you have? If so, you are on your way.

Given the fact that you have acquired practical knowledge, you have arrived at point B in your career as a filmmaker. That is, you have a fairly well rounded background and understand exactly why films are made, not the artistic experimental film you made in school, but the films people buy. Can you progress to point C? Can you accept a world that has not fully made the transition from print to nonprint communications? You may understand the impressive efficiency and high-sensory impact of audiovisuals and films, but you must never forget that the average person views film solely as a form of entertainment. Even at this late date, typical businesspeople have a limited knowledge of film and its effectiveness. They have yet to be taught the medium. If you can educate them, you have reached point C.

Proceeding to point D, what do you know about distributing film? Are you completely familiar with organizations such as Modern Talking Pictures? If you do not know what such companies do, how they operate, and how much they charge, you have more homework to do. One of the worst things a maker of informational films can do is "hit-and-run" a client. Handing a client a can of film does not complete the job. You must know how the client can put that roll of images to work, and you must share this strategy in your original budget. If you do not help your clients with distribution (and generally they will need help), you are simply handing over a vehicle with no fuel in it. The film may end up on a shelf after only a few screenings, and you will have destroyed the possibility of repeat business for both yourself and other filmmakers.

It is true that editors are still learning their trades after twenty-five years. And directors continue to discover new techniques after three decades in the genre. In the film business, you never stop learning. With this realization, you are on your way to the starting line.

The Starting Edge

In my experience most applicants for agency production jobs possess single or multiple degrees in film, broadcasting, or mass communications. Unfortunately, most candidates lack the two most essential qualifications for communications film-making: the ability to write a script and a solid business and marketing background.

A student seeking a film degree should seriously consider taking sufficient elective courses in writing and business to qualify for an MBA program. A person with a marketing background who can at least edit a script has a chance to land a job. If one can write a good script based on sound knowledge of marketing technology, a job is probably waiting somewhere. An associate once conceded that he would rather hire people with marketing/writing backgrounds and teach them film technology than the reverse. I tend to agree. Business is an infinitely larger and more complex field. Agency filmmakers can always depend on outside resources for film technology but must do their own marketing.

If you are currently studying film technology or are in the field already but considering further study, the following courses will prove helpful:

    advertising theory
    advertising design
    display design
    creative writing
    screenwriting
    journalism
    public relations
    marketing
    sales promotion
    retailing and distribution
    business law

> copyright law and ethics
> management information systems
> market research
> marketing motivation and persuasion
> personnel administration
> personnel training methods
> sales training
> cost accounting
> data processing (principles and systems)
> computer programming

No matter what area of filmmaking you aspire to, the above curriculum is an excellent adjunct to your film background. It can often save you when all else fails.

In addition, remember what I said earlier: business films are where the action is. The field is wide open and growing. It will continue to grow as students who are experienced in the use of audiovisual technology replace business communicators who were weaned on outdated textbooks. Film/video is as fresh as today. It is fast. It has impact, stored energy, and utilizes more sensory input. For these reasons, business will continue to turn to video, film, and audiovisual media.

THE AGENCY OPTION

Among today's nontheatrical filmmakers, the title "producer" is becoming as vague as the once crystal-clear New York skyline. It can mean anything from filmmaker to backer or jobber. In the advertising agency, it formerly designated the person who had the television spots made, but this is no longer always the case. More agencies are developing in-house capabilities as films, video, and audiovisual media replace print in marketing communications.

The Agency Media Producer

In some medium-sized agencies, a distinction is made between media, or television, producers and nonmedia, or direct communications, filmmakers. The latter generally do not produce commercials although their films do occasionally surface on television as short subjects in a select pattern of theatrical distribution.

Television producers in the larger agencies tend to have their own pecking order with a personnel matrix as complex as that of any large corporation. With few exceptions the smaller agencies offer much greater latitude for people who want to do their own thing, sort of. I say "sort of" because a client still must be satisfied as well as a creative staff of copywriters and art directors, their supervisors, and the account people. These people can hassle the filmmaker or media producer, but they are not of the same ilk. Each has a specific language, as does the filmmaker.

The large agency television producer is responsible for commercials and usually has them made in production studios. Although the cash rewards in this field can be great, there will seldom be much personal creative satisfaction. It is a job best suited to the filmmaker who has an administrative, as opposed to a creative, orientation. Nevertheless, while not required to be personally creative, the administrative producer must know and understand how to deal with the creative personality and mentality. If agency work interests you, be sure you can evaluate yourself on this basis.

Television producers working for small agencies will generally work on smaller accounts with respectively smaller budgets than their large agency counterparts. Spot producers working for small- to medium-sized agencies may do their own shooting and editing and will certainly handle their products to a greater degree than their big-time colleagues. The local spot producer is even more involved in the technical work, sometimes from the point of assigning storyboards through final viewing and approval of answer prints. The small agency producer will also handle radio spots, whereas such work is departmentalized in a larger shop. The trade-off is less money and pressure for greater individual expression and a more relaxed atmosphere. Nothing is being implied here; there are filmmakers suited to both situations.

Direct Communications Filmmakers

The second field open to agency filmmakers, nonmedia or direct communications filmmaking is growing slowly but steadily. Here filmmakers can often work almost alone if they are good enough, and unlike their distant cousin, the in-house filmmaker operating from the basement of General Bombastics, Inc., they will have an adequate budget. The field also offers many rewards to the business filmmaker. Production companies like Jam Handy, Wilding, and MPO, which pioneered communications filmmaking, have been the training grounds for some of today's established filmmakers.

A trend has been established today for agencies to offer more to a client. In the past, it was enough simply to place a certain amount of advertising in strategic media. Companies, however, are rediscovering that advertising campaigns must be reinforced by solid sales promotion and merchandising. Such programs are best produced by a single creative group to avoid needless duplication and maintain campaign continuity with an integrated marketing strategy. Although the logic of this backup approach is understood, too often the campaign flounders at the marketing level. A beautiful print ad that stimulates interest is useless without further literature on the product and a sales representative available for quick follow-up.

The agency that houses a resident communications film-

maker will also offer clients across-the-board marketing communications services. This will be neither a "boutique" agency
nor a creative consumer house handling cosmetics, food, and
cigarette accounts. Only a few of the large agencies have developed these true collaborative or direct communications
divisions. A fertile ground for the marketing communications
filmmaker, this field offers the greatest opportunities for students now churning out their great school epic.

Film plays a wide and varied role in the marketing mix.
Films are used in public service and other public relations,
sales promotions and meetings, trade shows, shareholders'
meetings, personnel training and orientation, retailing at point
of sale, and more. Shot in 16mm or videotape for one purpose, the marketing film often is sent to the reductions lab for
conversion to Super 8 continuous-loop cartridge for rear-
screen display or 8mm video for meetings or point of purchase.

In short, the agency nonmedia filmmaker will often handle
the full gamut of multimedia production: films, audiovisual
communications, disc recordings, slide shows, cassettes, filmstrips with and without sound, and videotape. It is a virtual
tour de force for the creative visualizer.

The Agency Film: A Scenario

By now the multiple levels at which the agency producer
operates should be apparent, but I offer the following case
history of production of a sponsored film, taken from my own
experience, to bring home the point. For emphasis, the producer in this saga is you.

The account executive, after consultation with his account
ad manager, calls and asks for a meeting. His client has a
problem that might be solved with a visual presentation. In
any event, he has run out of ideas and needs a specialist.

The meeting is held, but the account executive lacks facts you need to evaluate the problem. You decide to meet the client for the first time over lunch. Although nothing substantial is accomplished at this first client meeting, you now know the client a little better and can size him up for approach and handling. You have also monitored his reaction to you. And he owes you a lunch.

You set the second meeting for early morning over coffee so you will both be on the ball. At this meeting you discover that your client is licensed to sell a foreign-made vibrating pile driver that is ten times faster than the steam hammer and is virtually noiseless in driving caissons fifty feet into the ground. Your client has been flying prospects around the world to display this miraculous machine at work. His problem is how to get more exposure to his market. The solution seems very obvious to you because you have a cinematic orientation. The client does not.

You propose a short film showing four different locations and applications of the machine, or different models of the machine, at work. He wants to know how much it will cost.

Although you will need to quote a ballpark figure, the filmmaker who tosses off figures based on so much per foot is always making a mistake. So you follow up your quote by offering to prepare a proposal based on your approach to the problem. The client agrees.

In the proposal you write a rationale for the film, indicating how the product will be displayed in the film and how the client will benefit by using the film. You also include a distribution pattern.

When the client reads the proposal, he tells you he will never get this budget approved. Having anticipated that very problem, you zap him with a study comparing the cost of squiring prospects around the globe during one year with the cost of the film and its distribution.

The client is amazed. The film will actually cost less than 20 percent of last year's product sales presentation budget. He has to fight tooth and nail with established forces within the company, but he gets approval for the film.

Meanwhile, you realize that you can reduce the film to Super 8 and put it into a salesperson's projector for automatic showing on a continuous-loop cartridge. You also determine that the client's product is indeed news, so you offer the client twenty one-minute prints of a silent newspeg coupled with a one-minute news writeup that you will distribute yourself to television news directors in the client's choice of markets. You realize you can make this from your outtakes. The client buys it for an additional $3500.

You now write a script for the film that will be narrated over the footage and a second one-minute script for the television newspeg. When the script is accepted, you get final budget approval on the film and produce it.

The film produces under good conditions, and you show your interlock on deadline. Some minor changes are necessary, but you are still on the line because you budgeted carefully, allowing some margin for changes.

You are now faced with the arduous task of training the salespeople to operate a Super 8 projector or portable video cassette recorder. You carefully select one that is widely available and has a low breakdown history. You also arrange for continuing service on the projectors with a reputable equipment supplier.

You have now been through the projector so many times you feel you invented the machine, but your demonstration is a success and you have also made a few friends on the side. Although the program is an outstanding success, you never hear from the account executive, but the client writes you a nice letter that will be useful on your next approach.

Experienced filmmakers will smile and say, "If only they

were all that easy." No, they are not all that easy. You may have a beautiful film, but unless it helps the client, you have failed. The better salesperson you are, the better writer and researcher, the more information you have about your client, the greater your chance for success. The formula is the same whether you are an agency producer or an independent filmmaker: preparation plus work.

2/STARTING UP

The day I met Collin was great only for Eskimo dogs; the city was buried under snow. Collin was looking for a job. I was an executive producer at a medium-sized advertising agency.

Collin was late for the interview. Looking out my window, I assumed it was the weather. The great elm tree that so often brought me peace and relief from job pressure was nothing but a vague shadow in a field of snowflakes. Momentarily, my thoughts drifted to California and orange groves. Then, the phone rang: Collin had arrived.

Collin was a blue-eyed, carrot-top kid, rangy with a bouncing gait that made his curly red hair resemble tangerine pudding on a spring. He crossed the office in two steps and sat down before being invited to do so; he seemed to be in motion even while sitting.

Collin wanted a job in advertising, he told me without offering a greeting. He had been a film/video major in college and

*had taken one or two advertising courses. Interesting. His
resume told me his only experience had been placing some
ads as the manager of a local Burger King.*

*We chatted a bit and I said, "Tell me precisely the type of
work in which you are interested." Collin's quick response was
that he "would make a good spot producer." He had a sample
reel of spots he had made in college. The reel, he claimed,
smiling broadly, "contained some of the best ads, better than
those you see on television." Collin had a nice smile: a good
thing to have when you do not know what you are talking
about.*

*As it turned out, Collin knew very little about how an ad
was produced. He knew next to nothing about the local freelance talent and production shops that agencies rely upon for
television broadcast. He was ignorant of the inner workings
of an advertising agency. I told Collin all this and added that
his picture of the advertising business was as clear as my vision
of the elm outside my window, still veiled with snow.*

*Because I have never understood those who do not take the
time to tell, I told Collin that his unpreparedness rendered the
interview a general waste of time. "There are too many others
who have done all their homework before they come for an
interview," I said. Attempting to soften this jolt to his confidence, I suggested that he consider seeking work a serious
game. A game with rules. In games, you are competing with
others, so you figure out what you have to do to compete well
and then you prepare. The same basic tactic must be used in
the job game.*

HANGING OUT YOUR SHINGLE

Some of you may have apprenticed to accomplished and
established filmmakers; others may have graduated from a

film school or have earned an academic degree in filmmaking. Whatever your experience, you are currently frustrated for one of two reasons. Either you cannot land a job anywhere despite your willingness to sweep the floors for free the first year, or you already have a job but would prefer to work on your own for reasons related to individual style or life objectives. In either case, you have decided to make the big leap into independent production. But how do you get started in the world of filmmaking or audiovisual production?

Establishing Credentials

The first step in getting your business started is to establish yourself as a business entity. This can be accomplished by incorporation, which offers certain tax advantages and legal protection from libel. For most one- or two-person production companies planning to use freelance crews, however, incorporation will be a waste of time and money. Instead, you can set up in business by filing a DBA (Doing Business As) form with your county clerk. This process generally requires nothing more than recording the name of your business with the county. You can use your own name but I would recommend using a catchy name with a film theme until you become better known.

If you think incorporation may be to your advantage, by all means investigate your options. A corporate lawyer and accountant will be able to provide invaluable advice, although you do not necessarily need an attorney to incorporate. Their combined knowledge and your own professional goals should permit you to judge whether incorporation is appropriate.

After selecting a name and registering as a business, your immediate needs are a phone listing, business cards, and stationery. Get the first by calling the business office of the local telephone company. Explain your situation to the service

representative and request information on telephone company business accounts, various types of listings, and rates for
Yellow Pages listing. Also ask for information on listing services in nearby cities or communities.

When your telephone is installed, have a printer make up
500 business cards that include your name, address, and telephone number. If you can afford it, have a local art studio
design an eye-catching logo or select a distinctive typeface for
your name. They will provide camera-ready art for the printer
and can also prepare mechanicals for letterhead stationery,
envelopes, invoice forms, and notepaper using the same design. Initially, I suggest you order only business cards, letterhead, and envelopes from the printer. You will need stationery
to solicit work by mail and answer correspondence; for billing, simply type INVOICE across the top of the letterhead. The
time to print special invoice forms is after your business is
established. It is always wise to keep costs at an absolute minimum in the beginning.

Determining the Direction of Your Business

It takes an organized individual to succeed in business, and
organization extends to determining the direction a business
will take. Now that you have your business identity and rudimentary supplies, your next priority is deciding what kinds of
films you want to make for what group of clients. Once you
have made your choice, work hard to develop it.

This first decision is an important one, so take your time
and select one area of filmmaking to pursue. Go with your
strengths. A multimedia specialist, for example, has a brand of
creativity quite different from that of the advertising spot director. The former is experienced with a wide range of electronic hardware; the latter is skilled at making the most of tight
time constraints. Although these areas were once handled by

the same group of people, they are now so complex that they have become exclusive of one another. Specialization is the norm; therefore it is essential that you choose a single field and work at it diligently until you become known in that field for your outstanding work. After you are thus established, you can then expand into another area.

Selecting Equipment

Now the adventure really begins: you must invest some capital in equipment. What type of camera will you need—16mm or video? Although it is true that the best cameras are usually the most expensive, beware. Do not purchase a camera simply because it is loaded with features. Why buy a camera with a built-in intervalometer if you are not going to use it?

Before purchasing a camera always check on the availability of service and parts. If there are other professionals in your community, solicit their personal recommendations and advice. It is worth it to research thoroughly. After all, a used single-system camera will cost more than $1000; a double-system rig with motorized zoom lens and sync tape recorder, significantly more. Comparison shop, but keep in mind that negotiating for price may be easier with a large dealer who does high-volume business.

Next you will need sound equipment. At least in the beginning, it is easiest to opt for a single system. Buy magnetic striped stock, shoot it silent, edit, then transfer a mixed soundtrack from ¼-inch tape onto the edited film. Use ¼-inch tape because it is the sound standard and even the smallest sound studio can mix to ¼ inch.

You can devise a fairly inexpensive mixing rig if you put dreams of an expensive tape deck aside. Considering your present needs, you cannot justify that kind of expense. A used Sony TC 800B, for example, is not only a fine location recorder with the proper mike, but several can be put in tandem or side-by-side for mixing, along with a quality mixer like the MX–14. The Uher 100 is also an excellent choice. If you work in video, the one-piece single unit Camcorder, available in most formats including 8mm video, is the most portable unit.

Equipment rental has become an increasingly popular option for filmmakers, especially those just getting started. Renting equipment allows greater flexibility and minimizes overhead cost and the need to invest capital. Subdue your appetite for fancy equipment. Keep it simple at first; work hard and you should be able to buy the expensive equipment later.

Invoicing Your Jobs

You are in filmmaking to earn a living, so you must understand how to bill your clients before you approach them. Always get your business transactions in writing. Your client will probably require a contract, but if not, insist on one in a businesslike manner. Film equipment dealers carry contract forms that can be modified to fit your operation. You can also devise one yourself. Just be certain that your agreements are in writing and signed by both parties.

Two standard methods are used by filmmakers for billing sponsors or clients. One establishes four invoice periods: the first payment is due upon assignment of the project; the second after the script is approved by the client; the third at the interlock phase, or when the A&B rolls are approved with the soundmix; the final payment upon approval of the final answer print or delivery of the first release print. The second and more commonly used method is billing in thirds: one third due upon receipt of the go-ahead or purchase order; a second upon approval of the interlock by the client; the final third upon delivery of the answer print. In both cases, any client changes, such as modifications on the agreed script or interlock at the shoot or after, should be invoiced at above and beyond the established contract fee.

There are sound reasons for billing in thirds. The first payment provides you with advance money to hire subcontractors, purchase raw film stock, and rent equipment; the second payment is invoiced to acknowledge the client's approval of your work; the final payment not only approves the final answer print, but removes you from responsibility for print quality from that point on, unless you contract separately to deliver a definite number of prints or all future prints.

Distribution

Supplying a number of prints or videocassettes upon request is one part of distribution. Although distribution is not truly the filmmaker's area of expertise or operations—most turn to professional distributors (see source list)—some filmmakers do accommodate their clients. Helping your clients beyond the production phase will indicate your interest in their welfare, thereby establishing a strong, trusting relationship and enhancing your reputation.

Distribution should always be covered in a separate contract unrelated to production. Additional income can be made from print orders; be certain to scout photo labs carefully prior to ordering prints and get competitive bids for footage whenever possible. You should be able to suggest a sensible initial print quantity to the client if your distribution plan is based on a review of the film's objective and intended audience. Despite the attraction of getting reduced cost per foot if large quantities are ordered, keep the print order within reasonable and studied numbers. Extra prints sitting on shelves collecting dust are constant reminders to your client that someone made a costly error. Such mistakes harm you as well as other filmmakers.

THE SAMPLE REEL: YOUR FIRST JOB

Your business preparations are almost complete: you have established a direction, purchased equipment, and explored standard administrative procedures. You are ready to seek a client. First you will need a sample reel of your work; few prospective clients will want to pay for an intangible product by an unknown.

If you have apprenticed with someone in the profession or worked in an agency, your path may be somewhat easier; you probably have a small corpus of work from which to compile a sample reel. Be careful to keep your samples short whenever possible. Most clients have neither the time nor the patience to sit through a thirty-minute plant tour film, even an award-winning one. If you have something unusual that is lengthy but shows exceptional filmic skill, just pull out one or two of your best sequences. When you solicit spots, do not show anything but your own spots, and then only a few of your very best. Since the client will assume that you are displaying your finest work, be certain that you do.

If you are just starting out or are not exceptionally proud of your previous work, now is the time to consider producing a speculation film. Some filmmakers develop a speculation spot using an imaginary product or service. Others produce a spot for a well-known product and send it to the advertising agency handling the product, hoping to impress them enough to land an account. Another option is to create a film on speculation for a prospective client and then try to sell it to the client if the film is well received. Each option represents a great financial risk on your part, since you will not be reimbursed if the client does not buy. At least you will have produced a sample film; if you sell it, you will also have a reference from your first client to show to your next prospect. Do not just sit there with your video gear (or rudimentary 16mm) wondering how to get off the ground. Make a commitment and then adapt the following advice to your own situation.

Selecting a Market

Think market. The following example illustrates an obvious market for filmmakers: a dealer in large equipment. This dealer needs a film. In fact, he needs a film every month or two. Why? Because he has a huge customer list with varied needs. He currently depends on a handful of poorly photographed brochures; action motion picture footage would enable him to reach his market more effectively. Your job is to present this concept to him and to show him how a good film can save him time and fuel by making fewer product demonstrations necessary, thus increasing sales.

Now that you have chosen a market, you must canvass the lucky company. Avoid asking your prospect whether he wants to buy a film; the answer will invariably be no. Instead, explain that you wish to use his company as an example on your sample reel. Why? Because your sample will provide other businesses in your area with the chance to evaluate a time-proven method of demonstrating products and services. You merely want to film his operation and show your prospective clients the effectiveness of demonstration on film and how it can save them time and money. Customers can be shown a film of several pieces of equipment in operation without ever having to leave the office. Remember, right now you only want his permission to film. After you have produced your sample, you can attempt to sell him the completed film.

Some Preproduction Tips

The impact of a professional voice and soundtrack will be beneficial in selling your film to prospective clients. Therefore, it is wise to invest in voice quality. Do not go to a talent agency but try approaching a good college actor or perhaps a voice you like on local radio or television. Such a person may be willing to do your film voiceover on spec (deferred payment when and if the film makes money) or for a low fee the first time out. (Voices start at around $50 an hour and climb —especially when agented—to over $2000.) Consider placing a classified ad in the newspaper. The most successful producers generally select specialized talent for specialized jobs. Some scripts demand voices that convey humor, whereas others require authoritative deliveries. Take your time in selecting the right voice; the time will be well invested.

Once you have chosen the appropriate voice, have it professionally recorded. Talk to your local sound studio and develop a rapport with them. Nurture a long-term relationship and negotiate prices. Occasionally a studio will throw in a quick mixdown for you if you have all the elements tucked under your arm when you take your talent into the studio for recording. So, be prepared. Keep costs low by recording short sequences of informal narrative with plenty of space between complete thoughts. This will enable you to bring up background music during the pauses. The mixed track can then be transferred directly onto the magnetic stripe stock by connecting your tape recorder to your sound projector—if it has a sound record mode. This method provides plenty of margin for alignment and decreases synchronization problems.

A sound caveat (excuse the pun): do not use commercial recorded music for background. The 1972 sound record copyright law prohibits the copying of commercial sound recordings for this purpose. Producers must either contract for use of resources sold by a local audiovisual dealer or turn to commercial sound and music libraries. Such libraries are advertised in most trade magazines and provide the purchaser with original material released for low-cost use, music in the public domain, and standard sound effects. Building your own sound effects library is a good long-term investment, and the cost need not be high.

Budgeting Your Film

Prior to beginning any film, whether it be a sample or a sponsor-contracted film, prepare a budget. What is your time worth? What should the budget be? Some producers may take as much as they can get away with, but that type seldom stays in business very long. You are, foremost, a businessperson, and secondly a filmmaker. Your profits might derive from a 15 to 20 percent commission on everything you buy and handle during the project (such as film stock, equipment, set) plus a set hourly rate; you may also negotiate a package deal based on your estimated cost of operation.

Average hourly rates vary depending on geographic location. Naturally, you cannot charge inflated New York prices if you do business in Lansing, Michigan. Therefore you must set your rates for time and services based on three variables: what your competition is charging; the costs of goods and services; and how you rate yourself professionally. Are you just starting and learning on the job? Or will you be doing a fast and slick job, knowledgeably cutting corners while maintaining quality to save your client money? In the latter case, you should be earning more than the neophyte. Rate yourself honestly and sell your time in the area of $20 to $45 per hour.

Organize your budget using the sample budget log as a model:

SAMPLE FILM PRODUCTION BUDGET

Production Expenses
 Film stock or tape $____
 Sound studio rental $____
 Sound effects; music $____

Talent	$____
Mixing	$____
Processing	$____
20% commission on purchases	$____
Time (billed at hourly rate multiplied by time)	
Meetings	$____
Scouting	$____
Scripting	$____
Camera and support crew	$____
Sound studio direction	$____
Editing and postproduction	$____
General production management	$____
Miscellaneous	$____
Insurance	$____
Subtotal	$____
20% contingency	$____
TOTAL	$____

Again, you will have to estimate what to charge and make personal allowances. At this point in your career you may choose not to charge for meetings and scouting, but on complex jobs where those items eat up valuable time you should itemize them. If you hire a scriptwriter instead of writing your own script, itemize this cost as a production expense; you are also entitled to a commission on it.

Bear in mind the following budget tips: When purchasing film stock, allow a five to one shooting ratio; if you are planning a five-minute film, purchase twenty-five minutes of stock. Sound effects and music can cost $30 per needle drop or more. This is where investment in a sound effects library can save money. If you do not have a mixing facility, it will cost $45 or more an hour for studio time. When you can do your own mixing and cartridging you should itemize them under time.

Two places in your budget are appropriate for miscellaneous expenses. The first—clearly labeled miscellaneous—represents nonitemized production expenses such as travel mileage, tolls, and lunches. Keep receipts for these items. The second nonitemized entry is general production management time, under which falls all time spent on phone calls, making purchases, and handling materials. Although you can only estimate such items on your first budget, they represent valid costs that you will need to recoup. Your accuracy in anticipating these expenditures will improve with experience.

Insurance is definitely not an item to overlook. It is absolutely necessary that you insure against personal liability and against loss of production costs. Call local insurance agencies for a reference to a broker specializing in insuring filmmakers.

The contingency percentage (anywhere from 10 percent to 20 percent depending upon your client's ability to acquire funds) is strictly to cover yourself in the event of an unexpected rise in expenditures caused by runaway inflation, a bad accident, or any other unanticipated event. Acquaint your client with this significant budget item. Also advise your client of the slight possibility that the contingency might rise above 20 percent in the event of calamitous unforeseen events.

This additional fund is not yours to keep if unused. If you have brought the production in under budget or at budget, the contingency fund returns to the client if it has been advanced to you. Most clients, however, will not advance it but hold it for its purpose: a contingency against emergency.

If this is your first film for profit, you may look at the bottom budget line and feel it is too high. Consider your client's budget and sales projections. If your film stimulates ten times its cost in additional business the first year—and perhaps more the next because of increased exposure—the initial expenditure will have been a wise investment indeed.

The Script

You have reached the final step before production: the script. Begin by drafting out a tight script that contains only factual information about the equipment and sets up the shots. Then, if you are a good writer, embroider your subject—but use restraint. If you are not and never will be a writer, locate and hire one. Check the Yellow Pages under writers or copywriters; ask local newspaper editors if they can recommend any freelance writers. Scout nearby colleges and night schools for instructors who teach scriptwriting. Do whatever is necessary to obtain a professionally written script.

There are several excellent books available that detail the mechanics of scriptwriting and offer annotated examples (see Bibliography). For our purposes, the following script of the opening of our sample film will get the cameras rolling:

SCENE 1: Establishing shot:
Exterior of Agway equipment
dealer's showroom. ZOOM
SLOWLY FROM FRONT DOOR
AND PAN TO ROW OF FARM
IMPLEMENTS

                    Music up and falls behind
                    narrator. NARRATOR: Central Agway has operated out

of 2000 Elm Street since the days of Franklin Delano Roosevelt. Over the years their reputation for service has become known throughout the county. (two-second pause)

2. SLOW PAN ACROSS LOT
FROM HIGH POINT OF VIEW

Farm equipment sales represent just one division of the large Elm Street Agway dealer. Let us look at some of the Agway products and services that can benefit you. (one-second pause.)

The script continues to display three or four products and services provided by the dealer. It need not be overloaded with words or effects. The combined impact of action film and sound will sell the products—and the film.

Production Steps

You are now ready to shoot. The following checklist should help you get your sample reel produced and ready for viewing.

1. If the film is not a pure documentary, scripting is done first. Otherwise, scout locations prior to scripting. Take meter readings at each site; make careful notes on angles.

2. Draft a good shooting script based on logical continuity and highlighting benefits.
3. Select crew and talent.
4. Film all sequences using the best possible exposures. Design your shooting schedule around efficiency, not continuity. Since film is almost always shot out of continuity, assign someone to follow continuity sharply. It helps to take instant stills to attach to the script.
5. For best results, have your film processed by a lab recommended by trusted associates.
6. Edit your film so that it makes visual sense.
7. Draft final script from your shooting script for studio recording.
8. Obtain rough timing match—film/tape—while recording narrative. Edit script further if necessary.
9. Prepare a good selection of light background music and appropriate sound effects.
10. Obtain studio soundmix, taking care not to disrupt the rough scene-to-scene synchronization of your final script (number 8 above).
11. Have an answer print made from your original film rolls at your local lab.

Sales Presentation

Your sample film is complete; now you can attempt to sell it to your client/prospect. We will assume that the film is first-rate. That fact alone, however, may not make the sale. Placing a reliable, easy-to-operate projector in your client's office might help clinch the deal. Prepare a presentation kit for your client containing brochures on various types of self-contained projectors. Some of these desktop units offer traditional large screen projection, while others feature rear projection on small pop-up screens.

Perhaps the most impressive projectors are those using continuous-loop cartridges. They are quiet and extremely easy to operate; one need only open the case and push the start button. Be sure to emphasize the ease of operation to your client; it is a strong selling point for both the projector and the filmed demonstration concept. If your client buys a continuous-loop projector, have your film loaded into cartridges by a local audiovisual lab or one of the national cartridge loading services.

I do not recommend using a continuous-loop projector for showing your own sample film for two reasons. First, open-reel projection is faster and more convenient to handle should the film break during your presentation. Second, it will be simpler for you to make any necessary deletions or additions to the film.

If using video, be prepared to display all formats, including 8mm videocassette.

Making your client's film is only half the job. Insuring that it can be properly displayed under the most favorable conditions is the other half. If he buys his projector directly from you and you take the sales markup, suggest that he obtain a service contract for it. In many cases he can take advantage of expedited factory service offered by the manufacturer.

Other Potential Markets

Whether or not you make that first sale, you now have a sample reel safely in the can and have survived your first sales presentation. What other businesses can you approach with the sample? Start with the Yellow Pages; you will find all types of potential business contacts for one-shot films. Contact the local chamber of commerce: they usually have lists of all member companies in the area. Although these lists sometimes cost money, they are highly useful.

Do not rule out larger markets. Auto dealers often display action films provided by the manufacturer's marketing division. Local dealers, however, may also sell specialty vehicles or trucks that have applications in the field—applications best demonstrated on film. Perhaps they want to show off their clean, reliable service departments. A film of the service crew at work will eliminate repeated disruption of their work, as well as the possibility of customer injuries and related lawsuits.

Use your imagination when looking for prospects. Cabinetmakers may want filmed samples of their work—major jobs that were done for out-of-town customers. Plumbers may want films of complex and unusual installations. Bakers of specialty wedding cakes may wish to demonstrate their craft.

Cost is the most common objection to using film. Try to start with low-cost offerings. Even if the budget is very small, you have the equipment and time, so use them to record different images for a variety of clients. Introduce your prospects to the use of film or video. When they realize its utility, impact, and immediacy, they will know it is worth investing in on a scheduled basis. One contact will lead to another. You may not get rich, but a good living is there waiting for you. Just reach out and grab it.

3/SELLING

We sat in a French restaurant a couple of blocks from the Film Center Building long after the lunch crowd had gone, long after the dinner tablecloths had been laid down. My longtime associate, Ernie—once a power in Manhattan filmmaking who was clearly headed for Hollywood with a great high-adventure property under his arm—was now folding.

"I'm through," he said for the fourteenth time, as if trying to convince himself.

"What about that book you were going to write? Remember, the one about editing called Making Ends Meet?" He shifted uneasily in his chair.

When we finally parted, I watched Ernie disappear into the dark crowd on the street. It was almost as if he had been swallowed up by the horde, which was so thick it had a life of its own. At the same moment, a young woman carrying a film can walked by briskly. Lively and ambitious, she snapped her *fingers as she walked. What a contrast to Ernie. He was de-feated; she was not yet acquainted with the word.*

To succeed in filmmaking you must never succumb to de-feat. Whether you are just starting out or are a veteran of many years, you must maintain a fresh and eager attitude in your approach to the work. Headhunters throughout midtown Man-hattan describe those with this ability as self-starters. If you are a self-starter, you are never truly unemployed. When you are not working for someone else, you are simply working for yourself. Your outlook remains positive.

Successful people do not look toward the outside world for incentive: they turn themselves on. It is simple enough. They have learned how to rev their own engines before hitting the track. If you have or develop this ability by using a series of positive thoughts, you will succeed in selling your talents.

THE BASICS OF SELLING

Understand from the very start that sales is not a dirty word. Good salespeople are honest, well organized, and masters of their trade. They are also experts in their prospective custom-ers' businesses. Astute salespeople plan well and know how much "sell" to apply. They know the difference between a hard and soft sell, and who gets which. Successful salespeople keep good records and understand the meaning of follow-through. They are sincerely interested in helping their cus-tomers and do not abuse their talents for persuasion. The work is hard, tedious, and—for those who cannot separate ego from business—often humiliating. Good salespeople are, however, among the highest paid professionals in business.

Nothing moves in business without first being sold by some-one. If you have ever taken a telephone order, do not assume there was no sell involved. The sell took place before you received the call. Perhaps your customer sold himself, but the sell was there.

As an independent filmmaker or audiovisual producer, you will be selling an idea rather than a product that can be seen and touched. Only after the idea is sold does the tangible product—the film—become a reality.

Techniques for selling the idea of film are presented in the following pages, along with a brief description of the three basic phases of selling: the *canvass* or solicitation, the *negotiation* or actual sell, and the *close*.

The Canvass

Canvassing is as tough as you make it or as much fun as you want it to be. If you assume at the outset that you are an intruder on your prospect, you will certainly fail at canvassing. Your prospect will sense your lack of confidence. Instead of perceiving you as an exuberant flash of dynamite, your potential client will consider you a waste of time. The sale will be lost before you utter a word. On the other hand, if you are convinced you can help your prospect sell a product or service because you are a good filmmaker, count yourself in as a canvasser. The image you project implies that you have done your homework and know how to ply your trade as a filmmaker efficiently and honestly. You can be trusted to use appropriate means to promote your client's business and produce a film for the smallest possible budget. That is really all there is to it.

The key to successful canvassing is confidence. You become confident by knowing not only your own business, but also your prospect's business and communications problems as thoroughly as you can. It is a simple process: All it requires is a willing attitude and a positive mind set.

How do you canvass? The success of your approach to a

prospective client will depend on your preparation for the encounter. You do not call your prospect and ask, "Would you like a film?" Instead, consider the following dialogue as one effective approach to an unknown prospect:

FILMMAKER: (Dials phone number, takes deep breath and smiles.)

PROSPECT: (gruffly) XYZ Corporation.

FILMMAKER: Good afternoon, this is Toonerville Productions. May I speak to Mr. Smith? (Your research has uncovered Smith as the sales promotion manager, public relations director, or marketing manager.)

PROSPECT: Smith here . . .

FILMMAKER: Good afternoon, Mr. Smith. My name is Paul Jones. I am the vice president of Toonerville Productions, and I would like to have a chance to meet you and tell you about our business. Can we have lunch this week?

Let us analyze this approach. Before he makes the call, the Toonerville representative assumes a positive attitude. Using an acting technique, he psychs himself positively by thinking of something that turns him on. He ignores the gruff reply he receives from his prospect and continues to stand his ground, remaining cheerful and courteous. He acts, does not react. Realizing that people can "hear" a smile on the phone and that emotions are extremely infectious, Jones keeps smiling and tries to infect his prospect with positive vibrations. He is soft-spoken but sure of himself.

Jones properly identifies himself and his company; he also gives his title. In many communication houses and advertising agencies, the title of vice president is used extensively, not so much for ego-boosting as to elicit professional courtesy from the client. A title indicates the caller's career stage and the importance of the business he conducts.

This first conversation is an icebreaker. The filmmaker does not attempt to sell anything: he has simply opened a dialogue between himself and his prospect. He therefore avoids giving the prospect a chance to say no. The only question he asks is in the form of a lunch invitation. An invitation to a stranger for lunch is best phrased in terms of sharing, although the film representative plans to pick up the tab.

You will note the filmmaker's invitation pinned down a definite time. He did not ask, "Can we have lunch sometime?" He knew the prospect could answer, "Yeah, maybe some-time . . . ," thinking sometime in the year 2800. Should the prospect respond, "Can't make it this week," the filmmaker is prepared with an alternative: "How about next Tuesday, or Wednesday?" Again our filmmaker is savvy. He knows the ad-vantages of offering two choices rather than one. When one choice is offered, the prospect can say yes or no; with two options, the answer no is farther away. He also avoids suggest-ing Mondays, which are generally rough business days. Typi-cally, the middle of the week is less encumbered, but take your prospect's business into consideration. If you pursue your invitation carefully and suggest a convenient time, the pros-pect will usually accept the date to avoid being discourteous.

When you ask for an appointment, do not accept a put-off. Be prepared to respond to the objection "We're not inter-ested." Consider the following rejoinders:

"You'll want to see my work in the event an associate asks you about local filmmakers at some future time."

"Let's have lunch anyway. You may be interested at some time in the future."

"I'd like to know more about your division and its market-ing/training efforts; maybe there is some way I can help."

"I'm very interested in showing you how ABC Corporation solved a problem using film after I offered them a choice of solutions."

Each of these responses meets two criteria: it is positive and it offers the promise of benefits. By answering objections firmly and positively while expressing an earnest desire to provide a professional service, you should be reasonably successful in arranging an initial meeting.

Although few sales may result from these first encounters, after the lunch the filmmaker and production company are no longer unknown to the prospect. A basic informational exchange is the purpose of the meeting, but if the filmmaker has done his homework regarding his prospect's business, he can usually suggest a filmic solution to one of the prospect's business problems during the course of conversation. Subsequent meetings and negotiations for a film can follow if the prospect is intrigued. If not, you have made your presence known and perhaps have planted a seed that will grow and bear fruit in another season.

Negotiation

After your initial meeting, you are in a better position to assess how film can help your prospect's business and to use this knowledge to sell a film. Does your prospect sell a piece of machinery that can be displayed on film? Is the company manufacturing a new product that needs to be introduced to its dealers? Has an old piece of machinery been given a new lease on life with a new type of application? Does your prospect provide a little-known service that needs more public exposure? Is your prospect aware of how little it costs to present a public service film on local television? Such information is the ammunition used in negotiating a film production.

Present yourself as a professional. A good filmmaker will assure his client that he is providing a service. All appointments should be kept punctually. If a delay is unavoidable, the client should be informed in advance. Paying attention to detail gives the impression that you are organized and will handle your client's affairs meticulously, as indeed you should.

If you are successful in selling the idea of a film to your prospect, the next step in negotiation is usually a presentation. The filmmaker will screen a good sample reel and is prepared to answer questions concerning the budget for each production represented on the reel. A vague recollection of a budget can destroy a prospect's confidence in the filmmaker.

Following the sample reel screening, the filmmaker will offer a formal written presentation if the client has agreed to accept one. This presentation, referred to as a proposal, usually contains the following: a statement of the problem; a rationale for the solution of the problem; the cinematic solution to the problem; a comprehensive scenario of the forthcoming script; plans for distribution of the film; a comprehensive budget (to first answer print) with a grand total figure.

The proposal is discussed in detail later in this chapter. For now, it is sufficient to note that a proposal should be flawlessly typewritten and put in a presentation folder (available at most stationery shops). For a professional touch, the firm's name, address, and telephone number—with its logo, if any—can be imprinted on the folder, or a label printed with the company name can be affixed.

If you advance a bid at this point, it must be very comprehensive, covering every step of the production. You must not only justify the bottom line against the client's expenditure, but you must also balance it against projected sales or growth of business. The client must know how the money will be spent.

If your proposed film is a public service film with a news angle, do not be timid about proposing that film clips or a story be offered to a local television news show, a local newspaper, or a trade magazine. Your clients' public relations departments will do this type of job, but be sure they are aware of the possibilities. If your client has no public relations staff, include public relations in your proposal. Also assure your client that a good distribution plan will be created for the film. If you do not want to be directly involved with distribution, acquaint your client with professionals in the film industry who can help.

In every step of the negotiation, the filmmaker's preparation will prove the key to success. Those able to combine knowledge of the filmmaking art with an understanding of the functions of advertising, sales promotion, and public relations in business, will undoubtedly find themselves closing a film production deal.

The Close

If your client accepts your proposal, you are ready to close negotiations. Never close with a handshake alone; even if you have a long-standing relationship with the client, you should formalize your agreement in writing. All business transactions should be finalized in written form. If the production is small, a comprehensive letter of agreement signed by both parties is sufficient. In all other cases, you will need a contract.

The contract is generally provided by the film production company. As discussed in chapter 2, contract forms are available at film supply houses but it is best to draft your own contract to suit your needs. The contract should detail precisely the terms of your agreement with the client, outlining not only the filmmaker's responsibilities but also those of the client. An attorney should review your contract design. In some cases, you will want an attorney to draft a separate contract for a specific client.

Follow-through

Once the contract is signed, your sales work is completed. Or is it? You are now dealing with a potential repeat customer.

Even if your clients never contract for another film, they have contacts in the business community. Their impression of you and your work will be what is related to their associates. Ask yourself, "What can I do to assure that my clients will sell for me?"

In following through on a successful sale, the first step is obvious: delivery of a first-rate product. After that, assure a continued relationship by calling the client occasionally. Inquire how the film is doing out in the field and what, if anything, you might do to assist him in distribution. It is not necessary to solicit repeat business directly. By periodically reminding your clients of your interest in their businesses and by keeping abreast of changes therein, you will be in an excellent position to negotiate when the opportunity for another filmic solution to a problem arises.

PREPARING A FILM PROPOSAL

Just as follow-through can assure repeat and new sales for the filmmaker, a well-conceived proposal can clinch a deal, providing your client with a clear picture of the finished product as well as justification of the expenses involved. Bearing in mind this important fact, let us take a closer look at the basic parts of the proposal along with an actual rationale for a film with a $90,000 budget.

Before we begin, be aware that what follows can serve only as a model. In most cases where a proposal is requested, detail is encouraged. Indeed, some clients weigh proposals by the pound. Such detail is most often developed in meetings with your client designed specifically to elicit the information required to add substance to your proposal.

Outlining a Film Proposal

Prior to drafting the proposal, take time to research your client's business. Evaluate the client's situation during initial meetings. Does the client have a problem? What is it? Does the client understand the problem and do you both agree on what it is? What are your objectives? Before you put a word on paper, you must feel confident that you not only comprehend the client's problem but also have a viable solution to it in the form of a motion picture. Only then should you proceed to draft a proposal incorporating the following four parts:

1. *Rationale*

   Define your problem. Although your client may have initiated the project, others might make the final decisions. Help your client and yourself by writing a concise rationale stating the fundamental reason for the film. What will the film do? Will it change the audience's behavior? Will it result in a change in the client's market penetration? How? Will it introduce a new service or product? How? What are the projected results of the film's use? In barest outline, a rationale should cover the following points: presentation of the client and definition of his problem; identification of the intended audience; the proposed solution to the problem; an explanation of why film is the answer.

2. *Treatment*

   A treatment is a very tight outline of the script and film (or in audiovisual productions, the visualized message). Determine how much can be spent on each aspect of the film before writing the treatment. If you are working with a small budget, forget expensive location jaunts. The treatment of a low budget film calls for crafty as opposed to lofty imagination. Include the proposed running time. Remember that films are for impact and should not be burdened with details that befuddle the viewer. Length should also be determined by balancing the film's concept against its budget.

3. *Distribution*

Suggestions for the film's distribution should be included in the proposal. What is the expected method of distribution? Will the film be transferred to videotape or Super 8 for salespeople's use in continuous-loop cartridge projectors? Will it be shot for 35mm blowup for theatrical distribution? Or will it be shot in 35mm and reduced to 16mm or transferred to tape? When you design and build a vehicle, which is exactly what a film is, you should know the distance and to what destination the vehicle will travel. Budget considerations also play a role here. The filmmaker must be able to predict not only the cost of distribution, but what it will cost to transfer a print to another format, film gauge, or electronic medium. If the film is to be used effectively, the client must know how at proposal time.

4. *Budget or Cost Estimate*

The final part of the proposal answers the question most important to your client: How much will it cost? Prepare a list of expenses based on your treatment. Determine the degree of detail your client requires in an estimate and prepare your budget with a built-in contingency for strikes, inflation, and natural disasters. If you need help, refer to the sample budget in chapter 2. When you have completed your draft proposal, do not be shy about discussing the proposal at length with your client. Where necessary, make changes according to the client's needs. After all, only client approval of the proposal will culminate in a signed contract.

The Rationale: A Professional Example

Although the client's first interest may be the budget, the rationale is·the real heart of the proposal. If the rationale argues its case effectively, the expenditure for a film can be justified in the client's mind before he reads the bottom line of the budget.

The following example of a motion picture rationale was written by John Hammond for a large northeastern farm co-operative we shall call Grange Farm Enterprise Service. The film was produced to be shown by the client directly to his audience and for airing on local television in a strategic Sunday afternoon slot.

PREMISES. The primary audience of the projected Grange Farm Enterprise Service motion picture has been defined as 30,000 large farmers in Grange territory, of whom 10,000 are currently substantial users of Grange products and services. In designing a motion picture for this 30,000-member "prime" audience, we feel the following premises concerning these individuals can and should be assumed: Anyone who has built and is successfully sustaining a large farm enterprise today is almost certainly an intelligent, competent individual. He very possibly could be realizing greater income from some other kind of enterprise if income were his only criterion of business and personal success. We assume the attractions of farming that appeal most strongly to him include the relative independence and self-reliance afforded by the farm enterprise.

SUGGESTED THEME. If these premises concerning our major target audience can be accepted as valid, we feel an effective theme for this film would be "Independence through Cooperation." More specifically, we contend that Grange Farm Enterprise Service is the first full manifestation of the true cooperative principle. The goal of the cooperative has always been the greater success of the farm enterprise, but up to now it has been manifested only in partial aids and solutions, such as the low-cost or quality-assured commodities.

Enterprise is the culmination of the cooperative—a dedication to the overall success of the total farm enterprise rather than merely seeking to improve isolated parts of it. Correlation and synthesis of the vast number of inputs involved in this total enterprise approach have been made possible by aggressive utilization of the latest techniques and tools of information technology and management science. In the face of the proliferation and growing complexity of farm information inputs, it is resorting to the help of information technology and management science that will enable today's farmer to remain his own man—to continue to make his own decisions based on better and more refined information and to sustain his independence through a pooling of resources with other farm entrepreneurs "to do together the things we individually cannot do (alone)."

SOME FACTS OF LIFE. To be effective and credible, this film must reach its audience in a context of realistic recognition of the way things have been up to now and their anticipated status at the time of the film's showing. Following are some of the facts that the film should recognize and address.

1. In attaining the size and strength inherent in having the resources to meet the needs of today's farmer, all agricultural cooperatives (not just Grange) have encountered a problem of alienation from their membership. Many farmers feel that size had led to a loss of consciousness of the basic purpose on the part of their cooperatives,

and that the co-ops have forgotten who is working for whom.

2. Today's farmer is caught in a withering cross-fire of reports and recommendations arising from the work of some 10,000 agricultural scientists and researchers. Some of this information is (or seems) contradictory: all of it needs correlation to the farmer's individual situation.

3. Farmers—in common with most individuals—generally misunderstand the role of the computer in management decision-making. They may resent a computer telling them what to do.

4. The Enterprise Service representative is a normal individual who possesses no extraordinary personal powers beyond good native intelligence and a conscientious resolve to make the maximum possible contribution to the success of his Enterprise Service clients. We should not make the mistake of inferring that the Enterprise concept relies for its efficiency on any fundamental internal change in the Enterprise representatives themselves.

COMMUNICATIONS OBJECTIVES OF THIS FILM:

1. First and foremost, to establish that the Enterprise concept is a major new phase and really the culmination of the cooperative movement—this time seeking to foster maximum success of the total farm enterprise rather than simply seeking to improve the economics of isolated sectors of it. This is what farmers were really seeking to do when agricultural cooperatives were started in the first place, but of necessity could deal only with the individual facets of their problems. The new "total" Enterprise approach has been made pos-

sible by breakthroughs in information technology and management science. (Our suggested title, "The New Field," alludes to the fact that Enterprise seeks to be a rededication to the original purpose of the agricultural cooperative.) It is a utilization of those management aids by the progressive farmer—made possible by the pooled strength of his cooperative—that will enable him to retain his individuality and decision-making independence in the face of the growing complexity and pressure for increased size that characterize farming today.

2. To make clear that one of the goals of Enterprise is to make the Enterprise representative more effective in the farmer-user's behalf by placing extensive information and information-analysis resources at his disposal, as well as by increasing his knowledge of the existence and use of these resources. The value of the representative to the farmer is as an information and consulting "terminal" plugged in more firmly than ever to vast data and analysis resources at Grange Headquarters.

3. To establish that the success of Enterprise Service depends heavily on the farmer-user placing complete confidence in his Grange representatives, and that he can do so with the same assurance with which he discloses personal financial information to his attorney, banker, or real estate counselor.

4. To convey that the role of information technology in general (and computers in particular) is not to "tell managers what to do," but to provide more highly refined information and staged series of

management alternatives as aids to more intelligent decision making by the farmer-manager himself.

5. To communicate unequivocally that Grange—as represented by Enterprise representatives through backup specialists to top management—regards itself as a new, fuller manifestation of the ultimate cooperative purpose: contributing to the optimum success of its member enterprises. This film should make clarion-clear that Grange, at least, is one cooperative that has not lost sight of its reason for being, and that Enterprise Service represents an opportunity for a new and fuller partnership between Grange and its members.

WHY A MOTION PICTURE? The effectiveness of this communication is going to depend as much on the portrayal of attitudes, apprehensions, empathy, dedication, the need for trust and other emotional elements, as on the conveyance of a good deal of factual material. It is difficult to conceive of any other medium in which the nuances of image, motion, expression, voice inflection, and visual and audio effects can be deployed as effectively—and as unalterably—as in a motion picture. Once complete, a motion picture will be a more "official" statement of the Grange's aims for Enterprise than could any other visual medium.

A motion picture encapsulates power, impact, life itself. It freezes a moment of time, retaining all the vigor and drama that was professionally designed into it to be retrieved at any moment desired.

If you have merely glanced over the preceding rationale, go back and study it seriously. Although a rationale does not have to be this comprehensive, it must reflect solid research and understanding on the part of the filmmaker. The rationale indicates the filmmaker's awareness of the client's problem and defines a solution. It also sells that solution using creativity and fresh ideas.

It should be obvious from the example that any proposal must be written in clear, precise prose. If you are unable to communicate your ideas on paper, hire a professional writer to translate your understanding of the job into a proposal your client will accept.

Above all, do not underestimate the power of a well-conceived and professionally presented proposal. It is the nucleus of your sell. Even if your canvass yields many prospects, only an effective presentation/proposal will guarantee a closed contract and the opportunity to follow up that initial film with repeat business.

4/CLIENTS AND CLIENT STRATEGY

Joe Smith is a good filmmaker. He works fast and well, coming in on deadline and under budget every time. Joe looks good, watching his diet carefully, selecting fresh vegetables, fruits, and grains with the precision of a Toyota quality control expert. Yet he does not govern the quality of thought he allows to flood his consciousness. Just when you think he might be on top of the world, Joe is depressed and withdrawn. He pursues negativism until it drowns him with anxiety and remorse. Joe feeds his mind with garbage.

Part of Joe's negative syndrome is his inability to think himself out of a small restraining circle; to reach beyond the abstract wild blue into the wild purple. The very answer to Joe's dilemma is often just around the corner, but he pauses and abandons his search out of sheer frustration. Always remember that your oasis may be just beyond the next hill, your next sale might come with your next phone call.

As a filmmaker reading this book, you and Joe share a common goal: to make money in film. Your success in this venture depends largely on your ability to attract clients. Fortunately, the range of clients available to filmmakers is diverse and constantly growing, but this increases the variety of sales tactics required to capture money-making contracts. You must know in what direction you are headed and keep your wits about you.

The selling basics described in the previous chapter will provide the foundation for most sales situations you encounter. What follows builds on that foundation by offering a description of three different roads to making money in film and a strategy for building your business in each area.

PUBLIC RELATIONS

If you are looking for a film career that offers a fair living without the complications of backbiting egos, complex production techniques, and excessive competition, you may want to investigate film public relations. Although traditional public relations relied principally on press releases and feature articles in the print media to inform the public of corporate developments or institutional problems and changes, recent awareness of the impact of the visual media has changed this emphasis and opened an area of opportunity for the independent filmmaker.

Although network crews and local stringers amply supply hard news, many local television stations are still delighted to receive short segments of film portraying corporate, institutional, or organizational news. Such clips are used to fill time requirements for local news and even otherwise unprogrammed time.

Public relations clips must have a news angle. A new product that expedites a manufacturing process is not newsworthy: it lacks direct public impact. If, however, that product directly benefits the public—by enabling the phone company to make repairs from headquarters and thus eliminate 85 percent of their service calls, for example—it is news and a proper subject for film.

Soliciting Work

To get started in this field, you will want to canvass both your potential clients and potential outlets. The business desk at your local library can help you compile a list of all the public relations agencies, corporate public relations departments, news bureaus, and television stations in your area. Begin with the public relations professionals. Spend several weeks meeting them, soliciting their advice, and exploring the possible opportunities for using film to deliver their messages. Then proceed to the local stations. Find out about their policies on filmed press clips/releases. Most will be willing to consider such offerings. If they are not interested, put them on a list to be contacted again after you have a track record. Their attitude may very well change.

When you have completed your canvass, ask for an assignment from one of the public relations pros who might have encouraged your endeavor. Your first job will probably come from a public relations agency, unless the director of public relations or public information officer of a large corporation in your area gives you the go-ahead.

Once you have landed a contract, it is your job to keep your client's interests in mind. This may be difficult, since public relations people are driven by everything from rampant self-interest and flat-out misrepresentation to solid devotion to trivia. You may be asked to film a spot about a product that insiders feel is newsworthy but you do not. In this case, you will want to check with your media contacts to determine whether your clip will get air time, and then negotiate. Savvy, tact, and your negotiating skills will inevitably come into play. You can avoid becoming a hired flack by exploring far-reaching areas and cultivating every public relations source that may hand you a story.

Production Tips

Before you begin your first mini-opus, be sure you understand each station's guidelines regarding clip lengths (usually short, but get specifics) and type of soundtrack, if required. For material submitted to a local news service, it is quite likely the news director will prefer no voice-over. In such cases, the film will be delivered with a written release bearing all pertinent information and the telephone number of the releasing party to be contacted for verification or further information. Knowing these broadcast requirements in advance can save you production time and money.

On any assignment, your job is to film the news piece in the most interesting manner possible. This is typically accomplished by portraying the actual situation using a single system and cinema verité techniques. You will want to use all the film tricks in your bag; a novel change of angles may add spark to an otherwise mundane subject. Remember, the creativity must come from you. Budgets will rarely allow renting copter-cum-mounts for aerials, cranes, or other fancy paraphernalia. On the other hand, do not overdo it. You are shooting for the nightly news, not Hollywood.

Any good single system film/sound camera can be used as the main gear for shooting public relations spots. In cases where lipsync is not needed, you can make do with a silent 16mm camera coupled with a sound recorder for background sound. Videotape or Super 8 with single system sound is also an option if you are working for a small television operation. A fair range of three hard lenses or a zoom in the 12–120mm range will serve you well. Keep costs for all your technical arrangements to a minimum.

Double system gear can be used but is unprofitable unless you find some way of resolving directly to a postmagnetized film track. It is also not recommended because it lacks the immediacy essential to this genre, and processing through to a projectable film/sound presentation is too costly.

If you are shooting news film stock for a specific television station and have arranged for the station to develop your film —a wise option if the story is fast-breaking—be sure to check if the developer has been set for forced processing. This is a common studio practice that allows cameramen to rerate their stocks for shooting in low-light conditions. Obviously, the availability of this option could affect your shoot.

Although we started this section by pointing out the money-making possibilities in public relations film, you should not plan on getting rich in this field. You cannot charge an advertising spot rate for news clips because public relations budgets are smaller than advertising budgets. Business generally believes that public relations is less effective than advertising, and thus feels it should pay less—and does. You should still negotiate a fair rate for your work.

The public relations professional you are working for will most likely place the film in the media. Should you do the placement you are entitled to a fee in addition to your shooting fee. Your compensation should be increased accordingly if you can successfully place the story with a national or international bureau.

One additional money-making avenue is open to the public relations filmmaker: a major film story can emerge from a filmed news release. Quite often a release may hold the grains of a story that can be developed into a ten- or fifteen-minute promotional film for the company. This will not only benefit the company, but it is also an added source of income and exposure for you. So keep your eyes open and pursue such opportunities.

Nurture your business by maintaining an extensive contact list. Befriend the media people (without ingratiating yourself) because they are your bread and butter. The XYZ corporation may be paying for your film, but it is the LMN media that give you the break by airing it.

Business will also prosper as your technical abilities increase. Study newswriting techniques and read everything you can about the public relations game. A good book on reporting will broaden your perspectives, although reporting is not your primary objective. The books on these subjects mentioned in the bibliography can be found at most libraries and are well worth your time. Unfortunately, very little has yet been written on film/video journalism.

The field of public relations film has yet to be fully exploited. The idea must still be sold not only to businesses and organizations with newsworthy information, but also to some segments of the broadcast media. The time has come for public relations film, and the filmmaker who can present the opportunities of this field properly—with patience and professionalism—can succeed.

YOUR COMMUNITY AS A CLIENT RESOURCE

Beyond public relations, every community has a second area of untapped prospective clients often overlooked by independent filmmakers: local institutions, government agencies, and community organizations. Hundreds of these entities exist and need to communicate with the public. However, they need to be informed how film can help them. And you must first make contact with them before you can sell your services.

Educational Films

Two potential markets are readily apparent in your community: educational and religious institutions. Although opportunities in these fields abound, we will consider here some of the limitations confronted by the independent filmmaker who would do business with these institutions.

The educational film market is largely based on curriculum trends in the educational system. Films that exploit these trends have a chance of success, yet even then the filmmaker can expect very little financial return. To become best-sellers, such films must be handled by a major distributor who will generally pay the filmmaker no more than 10 percent of his profits. If your film does poorly and the distributor nets $200, your portion will be a paltry $20.

The outlook is equally depressing if your film is a best-selling success. Suppose your twenty-eight-minute film sells 1500 prints and the distributor clears $200 per print. Your check will be for $30,000; yet the film quite probably cost more than that to produce. Meanwhile, the distributor has made $270,000. Despite the evident inequity of this system, distributors argue that they cannot stay in business if they offer larger percentages. This may be true; however, if you produce an educational film, attempt to negotiate a contract that scales your earnings to the number of prints sold—the greater the success of your film, the larger your percentage of the profits.

To produce a best-selling educational film you need to be aware of not only curriculum trends but also which films have sold and why. Two recent books by Salvatore Parlato, *Films Ex*

Libris and *Superfilms,* offer partial lists of such films, including award-winners. Your public library buys many of the best films and can also provide accurate information on which titles are the most popular.

Surprisingly few educational films are made by professional filmmakers, but if you are interested in this field, here are some pointers for getting started. Review current best-selling films at your local library. Choose a film topic that meshes with current educational trends. If you have no expertise in education or the film's subject, hire a professional to write your script. Keep the film short: research shows that teachers and students prefer films running eight to fifteen minutes. Long films are also more expensive to make. Enter your film at the American Film Festival run by the Educational Film Library Association (EFLA). A good rating here can greatly increase the film's chances for success. Send your prints to several distributors and try to negotiate a deal based on a sliding scale. Whereas it is true the distributor is gambling on your film, so are you.

The most positive breakthrough in the educational field—as in most aspects of filmmaking—is the development of videodisc technology. The low cost of producing a moderate quantity of these magical pieces of plastic imprinted with both audio and visual information will permit the filmmaker to sell directly to his audience, thus eliminating the distributor/middleman and increasing the independent's profit.

Religious Markets

Although Christian television viewing is booming and organizations like the Christian Broadcast Network (CBN) are prospering, the religious films industry does not offer a viable marketplace for the independent filmmaker. The genre is well controlled in terms of both production and distribution: Each large church has its own production facility that employs gifted members of its congregation. Other fine religious films are produced by the news departments of the television networks, but the shops are closed and offer few prospects for the independent.

For those who feel "called" to this type of work, consider working for a film producer established in the religious film field to gather knowledge about the industry. Or join a denominational production company. Once you have acquired credentials and developed contacts and a firm understanding of the field, you may be able to hang out your shingle. Consider also the subcategory of spiritual films, which are essentially nonsectarian and often secular in content. The old "Insight" television program, a half-hour show that illustrated reason and morality in everyday life, was this type of production. A continuing market can be found for inspirational films, and if yours is well-written and conceived, it could stimulate perennial demand.

The Community at Large

Although the money-making potential of the educational and religious markets is limited, less obvious markets in your community can be cultivated to generate a healthy income from film. Develop contacts at the chamber of commerce, the local advertising club, and the trade organizations. Present yourself initially as an interested individual rather than a filmmaker. Consider the crime reporter who gets his best stories by hanging around the police station and the firehouse striking up conversations. You can use the same tactics to determine where potential film business may be found in your community.

In some cases, a film will be financed by individual rather than organizational funds. A film that I produced called *Roch-*

ester, First Person Plural was made for the incoming president of that city's chamber of commerce. The film stated his philosophy and what he hoped to accomplish during his term, while enlisting support for his projects. It became the keystone of a new program that served the community well.

Aside from business organizations, attempt to establish contacts within city, county, state, and federal government offices. Consider the broad range of possibilities: the school board, armed forces recruitment center, sheriff's office, and department of social services. A complete list is readily available in the local government reference pages in your phone book. Also look into quasi-governmental agencies such as child abuse centers and libraries. Do not forget action groups like environmental protection organizations in the private sector. In each of these areas, the need for films exists.

When you approach an organization, ask them about community relations. Some will have a promotional budget and others, such as the library, might have a patrons or "friends" group with a budget that can be used for filmed communication. Many of these groups have never contemplated using film, so your interaction with them is crucial. Make yourself known to them and stress that your intention is to help by using the skills of your profession. When a communication need arises, your name will be remembered. Establish the network of contacts first; the opportunities to sell will naturally follow.

If you are interested in government jobs, be prepared to bid on each project. Your first step will be to request a bid application from the contracting agency. Then, using all your technical and business skills, you will prepare and submit a bare bones budget. In this game, it is essential that you have a positive attitude. Recently a filmmaker who works almost exclusively on government accounts admitted to me that he encountered little competition in bidding. That did not mean he did not carefully watch the bottom line; rather, he felt that few filmmakers bothered to submit bids because they assumed they did not have a chance. To say it one more time: You cannot make any money unless you get out there and try.

LARGE ACCOUNT STRATEGY

Despite the importance of contacts in attracting new business, most filmmakers err by relying solely on contacts or referrals to keep their businesses rolling. This course is inefficient and risky, yet it is pursued because it is easy. Successful filmmakers advance beyond this simple method to develop the obvious next step: a sales strategy. Indeed, if your sales target is a large corporation, a contact alone will not assure you a contract; only a carefully planned effort will allow you to determine and then convince your client of the important role film can play in attaining corporate goals.

Research

Before approaching any corporate contact, you should find out everything you can about that corporation. Quite often all the material you need is at your local library. After reading a corporate annual report, you should have a firm grasp of the company's product or service as well as an awareness of possible areas for corporate diversification and expansion. These facts are of particular interest to you since they will be the subject of corporate communications and some of that communication will be on film. If you do not have a contact, the report can also provide the names of potential contacts: the training director, advertising director, public relations manager. You may even be able to glean some information about your contact's educational and professional background.

While doing your research, bear in mind that the large corporations composed of multiple divisions producing diversified products—for example, General Motors or Lever Brothers—will have decentralized buying and budgets. Study each part of such conglomerates; film possibilities abound. A need may exist for a corporate orientation film for all employees, plus several additional training films specific to each division's manufacturing or service problems. These films, however, will be purchased by different executives, so you will want to find out who they are.

All research should be thorough and methodical. Commit yourself to legwork and time at the library. Quite often, a letter to a technical, trade, or professional organization can provide in-depth information not readily available at the library. In addition, do not hesitate to contact the company's public relations office for information. Such departments are pleased to provide information to prospective suppliers.

Preparation

Prior to approaching a corporate prospect, check your work samples and reels for length, quality, and appropriateness. Your research will be useful in choosing the right samples. As you determine your client's needs, you will want to specialize your reel for that particular function, product, or service. A training director will be unable to appreciate your genius as a thirty-second television spot wizard, nor will an advertising agency producer by impressed by your fifteen-minute film on breaking down a thermonuclear reactor. Using your knowledge of your potential client should allow you to prepare your reel and pitch to suit that individual's needs.

Approach

The course of the sales meeting will generally follow the scenario conveyed in chapter 3. You must always approach your prospective clients in a positive and professional manner. Avoiding the following situations will undoubtedly enhance all encounters you have with your clients.

Never underestimate your prospects' intelligence nor their understanding of what you do.

Never press on relentlessly. If a prospect seems harried or busy, conclude your phone call but try to contrive an opportunity for a second call in the near future. Know when to push and when not to push by being a good listener and observer. Watch for signs of fatigue in a meeting. Clock-watching is one surefire danger signal. Prospects have work to do and you are occupying their time.

Never deceive your client or prospect. If you have developed this style, break the habit before it breaks you. Deception, charming or otherwise, is poor cement in a relationship.

Never project a negative stance—whether it be toward the prospect's competition, an individual, or the state of the economy. Optimism is always best. Remember also the power of a smile.

Finally, avoid doing all the talking. Learn to be inquisitive and a good listener. It requires effort, but the information you pick up by listening could very well help you clinch a deal.

Follow-up

After your initial meeting, you should be able to determine the potential for film business within the corporation. In making your projections, consider the following factors: corporate growth during the past five years; net profits for the past five years; advertising and other communications expenditures for the past year; diversification of operations, products, or services.

Another variable is the relative sophistication of management in the use of new communications technology and the recognition of its importance. The filmmaker can help control this variable by educating management before selling. Quite often the manufacturers of videotape or a film distributor will share the expense and effort involved in this educational process. In other cases, your point might best be made by screening a successful sales promotion film produced for your client's competitor. The most difficult part of your job can be convincing your client of the impact of film.

If you determine that potential business exists for you in the company, draw up an organizational chart to monitor your various sales approaches. Include all corporate officers from the marketing director on down, drawing distinct lines up to supervisors and down to subordinates. Pencil in public relations personnel and anyone who does training. Under each name, place pertinent information such as phone number, extensions, and notes on personality. You will also want to keep a log of all phone calls to the company and note the results. Such steps can allow you to coordinate your sales approach to attract multiple contracts from a single corporation.

Throughout this chapter, we have surveyed potential markets for the filmmaker's work, but in so doing, most of the discussion has centered on business practices adaptable to almost any profession. Why? Because to make money in film, you must be a good businessman. Filmmakers begin with cinematic skill and talent. Continued success depends on detailed planning and careful handling of accounts. By marrying your art with sound business practice, you can make good films and a good living.

5/SURVIVAL

You can read all about the great directors almost anywhere today. They became great not by wearing designer jeans, nor by driving exotic cars, but by applying themselves. They made a commitment to dig in and work very hard at something they chose to do.

When as a young boy I first became enamored of Frank Capra's work, I knew very little about him. Actually, I would have had to search hard to locate the few articles that had been written about him; it had been a long time since he and the handful of greats—Ford, Wyler, Wilder, Stevens, and the rest—had made craft history not matched since.

Throughout my career, I honestly sought out the formula for greatness because like many other "little" people, I too yearned to be great. As the decades rolled by, I learned to distinguish greatness from fame and began to realize that the essence of greatness was intrinsic to each of us. It had to do with a fundamental concept so well defined by Capra.

In observing Capra's work, one cannot miss his underlying message. He actually gives it away in one of his films, his classic It's a Wonderful Life. *In it, the protagonist George Bailey's father (played in a brief role by the wonderful character actor Samuel S. Hinds) has the magic theorem written on a small plaque mounted on the wall behind his bank office desk: "The only thing you can take with you is that which you have given away." If the George Bailey character had discovered this (which was right under his nose) for himself, there would have been no story, no classic film, and the extraordinary James Stewart would have been out of a job.*

In the mid-1970s I had the opportunity to have dinner with Frank Capra and I listened to him with the reverence of a school child, noticing that within almost everything he said was a tidbit of advice or information. He never stopped giving. I asked him many questions but one lingers in my mind because of its significance: "Why did 'Gunsmoke' last so long on television? It was just another western, wasn't it?" Without hesitating, Capra said, "Because each week the audience was given a love story.... The protagonist loved his homestead, his horse, his little boy, and so forth. People love a good love story best."

Frank Capra knows much about love. His work reflects it from the very early silents to the feature films, World War II documentaries, and his early and extraordinary television series on science. His dramatic vehicles are all humanitarian.

Thus we come to the key to survival in this business and the solution to the mystery of greatness. Through our work, we give not only to others, but to ourselves as well. Surviving is easy if you bring love to your work. Greatness is measured by what you can give. Giving is very painless when you realize you are also a true recipient. This chapter helps both of us because it provides me with the opportunity to give. And the spirit of this chapter is part of the reason why this book is dedicated to Frank Capra.

Having read this far, you should have a good idea of how to get started as an independent filmmaker. You also may have a number of questions about the process. What follows is a series of frequently asked questions with answers derived from my own experience as a commercial filmmaker. They, in turn, are followed by a compendium of tips for surviving in the filmmaking business.

SOLICITING WORK

Q: I work in a small town. Since there are no labs here, would it be impossible to do professional work, even on a small scale?

A: If you say it is impossible, it will be. If you live in a fairly large city—one with a population near one million—that has no labs, cultivate the local television stations. Those that have not switched to electronic news gathering are probably equipped for color processing and small-scale editing. Otherwise, obtain a list of labs in neighboring cities by checking the Yellow Pages of those cities at your library or by writing to the Association of Cinema and Video Laboratories. Select several of these labs and write to them, explaining your needs.

If the response from a lab is encouraging, budget a trip to tour it. (The cost of the trip will be tax deductible if you are doing business in film.) Prepare a list of questions in advance. A good lab is always willing to answer its customers' questions.

Q: How can a lab help other than by processing my film?

A: Aside from film processing and printing, most labs can also provide information on camera equipment, editors, editing rooms, sound studios, special effects, and completion services. Be certain also to ask who is placing the largest footage orders. The answer could lead to a new client or a "big city" producer in need of your services.

Q: How do I solicit new business?

A: Besides those methods described in chapters 3 and 4, direct mail is an effective means of stimulating new business. Although it is expensive, some type of 3-D mail is most appropriate for film and audiovisual producers. (Refer to chapter 6.) Otherwise, it is best to be represented by a professional-looking mailing piece that has been well written—preferably with catchy or clever prose—and strikingly designed. You might wish to hire a copywriter, although you can do the writing yourself, and you should certainly enlist the services of a small art studio for the graphics. If this type of circular is beyond your budget, seek the help of a typing service. A well-phrased letter, neatly typed on your company letterhead, will also go a long way toward attracting business.

As stated previously, do not overlook the local television stations. Quite often they need both news camera operators and budget producers for retailers who buy spot time in your city. They may even be able to provide leads on local businesses—large auto dealers or furniture warehouse outlets, for example—who have requested production services.

Remember that regardless of where you live finding your market is fun. You will enjoy playing a sleuth, tracking down leads with clues, using your mind, and developing your skill at deductive logic. Do not assume that anything is impossible.

Q: Where do I find clients who are interested in communicating on film?

A: You should know the answer to this one already. Potential clients are everywhere; the only problem is that they are not always aware of their needs. It is your job to sell them on the value of film. The Yellow Pages is a directory of potential customers. Target those firms having the largest ads. Talk to business people about what you know best: film. Tell them about the benefits of film and be prepared to show them how film can save them money.

Remember that you must know your prospect's business before you attempt to provide a film to promote it. Let your prospect know that you are interested, ask about the business, and suggest that if you see a way to help by using film, you will propose it. If you discover there is no business for you, thank your prospect for meeting with you. All is not lost; you have made a favorable contact that might result in an indirect sale.

Q: I have a good reel of sample productions. By that I mean a single reel, and I do not want to risk sending it around. What do I do?

A: Every business, trade, or professional organization has an occasional need for luncheon speakers. Speaking engagements provide an excellent opportunity for you to present your sample in person. Offer to make a presentation on your services to the local advertising club or Rotary. Prepare an interesting talk. By keeping it brief and direct, you can increase your effectiveness and maintain audience interest. If you need an icebreaker, consider borrowing a comic short from the library.

Sometimes you will have to risk sending out your reel, since your work must be seen if it is to stimulate business. Consider making some ½- or ¾-inch videocassette duplicates for this purpose. Duplicates are quite inexpensive if you have a videocassette recorder; just purchase blank cassettes. If the duplicates must be made for you, the cost is still moderate.

MANAGEMENT DETAILS

Q: What is a simple way of budgeting a film?
A: Review chapter 2 for a detailed discussion of budget, but

in brief, there are two steps: 1) Compile a list of all production costs and mark them up not more than the agreed 20 percent for handling. 2) Charge for your time at a rate based on local cost of living. Quite often the individual project will determine your budget. On some, you can choose to forego an hourly rate and work solely for the overhead markup, whereas on more complex shoots with large budgets you may negotiate a package deal. You will have to judge what is right in each situation.

Q: I just lost a bid to another filmmaker. My bid was as tight as possible. How could he afford to underbid me?

A: Chances are that he could not afford it. You may have been underbid by someone who wanted to capture the account. The low bidder may then try to play catch up by increasing costs on any subsequent films he makes for this client. Bidding below your costs is unprofessional, and the end result is a less than quality film. On the other hand, if your bid conforms to costs and you come forth with a fine product, you may never have to submit another bid.

If you are really concerned about your competitor's low bid, call him and ask how he could afford to be so generous. If you both gauged your bids on a careful budget and a reasonable profit but his bid was just a few dollars under yours, he probably knows his business a bit better than you do. You will know better the next time.

Q: I understand that most large projects progress from proposal to script to estimate to production. Should I charge for a proposal?

A: If your client requested a proposal, you should indeed charge an hourly rate for preparing and writing it. You may choose to waive this fee when the proposal is the result of your suggesting film as a new technique to your client. If not, obtain your client's approval of the fee prior to billing.

Q: I just received a complex assignment and will need to hire a writer. What is their standard rate of pay?

A: Most writers will quote you their rates. You can also obtain rate information by contacting the Writer's Guild East or West, or by consulting the current volume of *Writer's Market* and issues of *Scriptwriter Magazine* and *Writer's Digest.* Writers charge either hourly rates or per page rates. In many cases, the writer will receive close to 10 percent of the total budget for writing a script through to final approved draft. An experienced writer who provides copy and script for advertising often charges $100 and up per approved typed page. Many audiovisual and videotape scriptwriters will work for much less. The trick here is to negotiate. Always carefully verify your prospective writer's references.

Q: How should I invoice the client?

A: As described in chapter 2, the current practice is to bill film jobs in thirds: one third upon script approval; one third upon approval of the interlock; the final payment upon delivery of the first answer print. If your client is a corporation or a large institution, obtain a numbered purchase order detailing the services and products you will provide. Place the purchase order number at the top of all your correspondence and invoices to identify them and expedite all administrative handling.

Q: Who owns the props, outtakes, and/or material used during film production?

A: It is an industry practice that all aspects of production are owned by the person who paid for them. Unless instructed otherwise, be sure that everything is delivered to your client, including the workprint. After the answer print has been approved, send a letter to the lab assigning rights to all property —such as A&B rolls, soundtracks, and negatives—to your client. Send a copy of this letter to your client; retain a second copy for your own files.

Q: Do I get my name on the credits of my production?

A: Credits for yourself and your staff may be included on the film only with the agreement of your client. It is best to negotiate this point as part of the contract. Avoid giving your client a credit as executive producer. It gives your client creative authority that may not be deserved.

Q: I made a film for a client, he liked it, and it won an award. But I never heard from him again. What, if anything, did I do wrong?

A: Nothing! In fact, that is the problem: You did nothing. Why do you feel that you should hear from him? After all, you are the one who is offering the service. Did you set up a good distribution plan for your client? Did you follow up on its use? Did you check back to see if there was anything you could do to help him? Or even call just to say hello? If you have not kept in touch, it could be that another filmmaker is harvesting the field you plowed and sowed. You had better pick up the phone right now.

STRATEGY

The answer to the final question above could just as easily have been included among the following tips on how to maintain and build your business once you get started. Following through on your last job should always be a top priority, but there are other ways to keep your business thriving. Consider some of the following tactics.

Take Inventory

Are you expanding your business contacts? Do you belong to any trade organizations? Do you attend trade shows? Search out opportunities to make business contacts. Mix and mingle; after all, this is a business of communication. In all too many cases, it is who you know that counts.

Devote some time to devising a public relations program. Are you listed in publications like *The Creative Black Book,* which offer free or inexpensive exposure? Attempt whenever possible to place your business name before the public at little or no cost. There are more opportunities than you might think.

Cut Down on Expenses

Whenever and wherever possible, keep your overhead low. If you have equipment that is mostly unused, you are wasting capital. Sell such equipment and rent it back when you need it. Do not let your ego run off with your business. Put cash in the bank for lean times. Too many former filmmakers bought hardware goodies to handle and show off. Do not join them.

What type of car are you driving? An expensive two-seater? Consider this indulgence. If you decide that you can really afford it, hide it from your clients. Many of them will resent it and will not care that it is a result of your success.

Think about all the places you can stop money leaks. Are you having lunch out most of the time? Saving even a dollar a day means $365 at the end of the year.

Organize Your Operation

Plan for the efficient employment of your personnel, if you have any. Teach a less than busy secretary/receptionist skills such as slide mounting or canvassing business on the phone. If you work alone, review how you spend your day. Is your day spent efficiently? Are you making new business calls? Schedule them. Opening roads to new business is just as important as calling on existing accounts. It is part of an efficient operation.

Diversify

What type of films are you making? Have you specialized in any particular field? If you have specialized in commercial spot production, remember that it is a trendy, fashion-conscious, highly political business. If the wave passes you by, you are finished. Protect yourself by diversifying. After you have become established in one field, go after other business whenever you can; at the very least keep your eyes open for other opportunities.

Diversification can be quite simple if you consider slide shows or filmstrips. Currently, slides are enjoying a great comeback. More companies than ever before are discovering that training and other communication can be best conveyed by audiovisual technology. In addition, companies are attracted by the modest budgets involved in using audiovisual communication as an adjunct to their printed programs. The average filmstrip or slide script sells for as high as several thousand dollars and basic photography (for audiovisual) is billed at several hundred dollars per day, so it is easy to see how your business overhead can be paid by producing one or two slide presentations per month. Take advantage of this trend.

Hybridize

A hybrid production is a combination of film and tape. If your production will end up on 1-inch tape or on videocassette, consider transferring your approved film take to tape and complete the postproduction on tape. By carefully planning your editorial time, you can cut the budget by one half this way. Just compare the cost of completion on tape versus film through wet and dry labs and tape edit. The savings may well be sufficient to purchase a tape deck and some blank cassettes.

Study the Business

To survive and do well in filmmaking, it is essential that you read books and trade magazines to keep abreast of all developments in the film and video industry. Right now video is in the ascendancy, but it will soon be bypassed by software currently beyond conception. This field is fast moving, and you must be aware of any trends that can affect your business.

Read every trade magazine you can find, paying special attention to the ads. Write to manufacturers for brochures on new equipment. Get on their mailing lists. Do everything you can to learn about new equipment or modifications to existing hardware that can change your business or expand your facility.

After reading this book, if you decide to use it as a handbook in getting started as an independent, return to this chapter to gauge your progress. Once you have grappled with most of the questions asked here and applied the survival tactics to your own business, you can count yourself a success. You will undoubtedly be making money in film.

6/PROMOTING YOUR BUSINESS

The young woman had large blue eyes and hair the color of unpicked corn in midsummer. She was Scandinavian and appeared to wear no makeup except for false eyelashes. As she moved in front of the camera, the crew worked to place light to make her hair gleam and enhance her features with softness.

Everything seemed to be going beautifully. Looking across the room, I caught the eye of the producer. He smiled and winked at me as if to say, "Everything is going very well. Hope you are okay." We were just about to shoot some expensive 35mm footage.

The producer was an old friend who had hired me to direct for him on other projects in the past. I signaled him to wait, walked over to him, and asked in a hushed voice, "Where is your still man?" He looked around and then down at the floor. "Uh, we have no budget for a still photographer . . ."

"But this is a new product," I said, carefully forming my words. "Didn't anyone from the client suggest still coverage?" He looked at me and again his eyes sought the floor as he said, "No, but I should have."

In overlooking the need for a still photographer, my friend failed not only his client but also himself. It will become clear as you read this chapter that he missed an opportunity to derive promotional material for his own business while extending the scope of his work for a client. The filmmaker who is also a canny businessperson will always be looking for such opportunities.

One of the keys to your longevity as an independent filmmaker will be your ability to promote and merchandise your services successfully and creatively. Several effective means of doing just that are the basis of this chapter. Although these tried and true methods can be valuable in locating new business, they are just a starting point: Only your variations will make a promotion work for you. Furthermore, some of the advice herein will sound familiar because it is an elaboration on the business basics discussed earlier. Clearly, practical application of the basics will be at the center of your success, initially forming the building blocks of your fledgling business and later the foundation upon which creative promotion is based.

HOW TO MERCHANDISE YOUR BUSINESS

Filmmakers presenting their services to prospective clients must create in each prospect a desire to see their wares. Prospects must understand that you have studied their communication problems carefully and that you are genuinely interested in their welfare. After all, the success of a client's business will mean success for yours as well. By carefully planning your presentation, you can nurture your prospect's interest in your business.

Before you think of contacting a prospect or old client about applying a filmic solution to a communication problem, be ready to reply to all objections. That means devising three answers to each anticipated problem. Since the usual objection is budgetary, be prepared to show your prospect how the extended use of film compares favorably in cost to another medium. The key, as always, is preparation, so let us review some of the basic steps from the perspective of merchandising.

Know Your Prospective Client

Who is your prospect as an individual? Study your prospect's habits, preferences, and dislikes. Would the prospect consider a hard sales pitch offensive? If you do not know, take the individual to lunch and find out. Do not be afraid to ask questions that touch on personal habits, although you should take care to place them in context. Always use tact and diplomacy. Every person has a different level of tolerance for probing questions, so try to communicate sensitively. Move the conversation away quickly from the weather and Saturday's ballgame and talk about business. Above all, however, listen to your prospect.

Once you know your prospect, you can cater to the individual's attitudes and preferences while merchandising your services. Point out that motion pictures, video, and audiovisual presentations have an extra dimension that results in recognition for those using these media. Drop an occasional hint about the visibility resulting from screened presentations.

Stress the cost effectiveness and memory retention produced by the multisensory impact of film. This is merchandising on the personal level.

Know Your Prospective Client's Company

Who are the employees? How is management arranged? What is the business history of the company? Who is their competition and how do they compare with the rest of the industry? How well do they communicate with their public? Have they commissioned a film production before? By whom? You cannot merchandise the company until you know the facts.

Determine whether your prospect's competitors have used film. If they have, point out the necessity of matching competitors in the marketplace. On the other hand, if the competition has not adopted film, argue the advantages of beating them to it. The amount of interest you generate about your work will infect the potential client, and thus the company. If you lack enthusiasm, so will your prospect.

Plan a Good Presentation

After you feel you know enough about your potential client to present your ideas, start planning. Remember to design the presentation around what you know about your prospect's needs. Think in terms of true benefits for your prospect, who is bound to ask, "What can you do for me?" You must provide a satisfactory answer if you want to be hired to produce a film.

Keep your presentations short, but be sure to present all your points. If you have made a film that relates to your prospect's needs, show just the first five minutes or so. Then turn off the projector and briefly describe the project's benefits. (If you are asked to show the rest of the film, great—but do not be crushed if a prospect cannot spare the time.) If a sales promotion film you produced enjoyed wide distribution, you should be able to acquire a history of the product's performance before, during, and after distribution. Present such findings to your client on paper. Quite often a satisfied client will be pleased to write a testimonial on your work. Do not be timid about soliciting such recommendations if they are deserved. Then use them to strengthen your presentations.

When you present a reel or cassette of television spots, use only your most exceptional and recent spots. Edit in only those spots that relate to the product or service family in which your potential client deals. If you have a particularly impressive spot—a big budget job or a Clio winner—try to determine its effectiveness. Solicit numbers from the market research people or advertising agency for whom you made the spot. Was there any measurable sales increase after the campaign? How did the spot pay off for the client? Clios are wonderful for your ego, but they do not impress smart clients, so emphasize hard sales data, not awards. Merchandising means talking performance.

Follow up presentations with a call or letter of thanks. A show of gratitude will go a long way to indicate your interest and sincerity. Potential clients do not like to feel they are being hustled. If you fail to win a job after a presentation, remain in touch anyway. Let your prospect know that you are available, ready, willing, and able to help with communications problems that can be solved with film. Do not hesitate to offer to screen another film if you think the prospect would benefit from seeing it. Such follow-through can go a long way in cementing a future business relationship.

DIRECT MAIL THE 3-D WAY

Canvassing is not the only method of getting your foot in a prospect's door; a direct mail campaign can be equally as effective. To be successful, however, your prospect must read your mail and react to its message. Therefore consider the power of 3-D campaigns.

Be honest. How much attention do you give to a letter hyping someone's business, even when it is expertly or cleverly written? Chances are such mail lands unread in your wastebasket. 3-D is something that comes in a box. It engages the receiver's curiosity.

Earlier discussions of direct mail stressed the need for color or an unusual graphic technique to arouse attention. If you can afford 3-D, however, it can even more substantially improve your recognition in the market. It also makes sense for a filmmaker to make the strongest visual statement possible.

There is some good flat mail that has character, pizzazz, or some utility. Consider the Fotomation film timetable or the small slating card sent by photoanimator Al Stahl of New York City. The timetable has a gauge/film footage scale lined up with seconds, minutes, and number of words per foot. I use these gadgets often and guard them with my life. Someday I will use Al's animation camera again because he is so clever with his direct mail and always delivers the goods. That is the crucial point here. If you are going to invest in direct mail— whether 3-D or flat—be prepared to produce results.

To illustrate the power of 3-D, let us study an extremely successful mail campaign devised by the Marsteller advertising agency for Clark Equipment Company. Marsteller called it, "the case of the two-pound calling card," and it ran as follows.

In 1964, six-year-old Clark Equipment was the country's fourth largest supplier of trailers. Their problem was that 300 major buyers did not buy from Clark and never had. The direct mail campaign was designed to establish direct personal contact with these nonbuyers.

The campaign began by sending off a chef's hat with this message: "Clark salesmen wear many hats—equipment specialist, financier, service man. A good reason to buy Clark trailers." A week later, three gourmet-style barbecue skewers were dispatched bearing the story that Clark had the right equipment to handle the customer's job.

Message three—also sent after a week—comprised salt and pepper shakers indicating that Clark had the extras that are important to trailer buyers. The fourth week a cookbook was mailed with a message about the firm's wide experience in matching products with customer needs. The next gift, a padded glove and apron, symbolized downtime protection. Clark had that, too: a nationwide service setup.

Each package and message was accompanied by a salesman's business card that said "stand by." During the sixth week of the campaign, a two-pound prime filet steak was delivered by the salesman in person. The message: "This is the kind of personal service you always get from Clark." Personal contact was established with 300 prospects and resulted in 50 new accounts. An investment of $12,000 had yielded $3.5 million in new sales.

This campaign illustrates the effectiveness of 3-D direct mail. In order for this concept to work, discipline is demanded on several levels: discipline on the client's part to reduce the prospect list to the smallest number possible, usually a few hundred; creative discipline to insure that individual pieces never become gimmicks and overpower the sales message; finally, the discipline to make follow-up research an integral part of each 3-D campaign to determine the return on the communications investment.

The average filmmaker soliciting new clients does not have the resources to mount elaborate 3-D campaigns, but studying such efforts can suggest some successful approaches. What can you afford in terms of 3-D? Start by checking out an advertising specialties company. Their staples are pens, desk accessories, and other utilitarian objects that carry a company name. Some creative houses will collaborate with a customer in devising a unique item that communicates and can be produced at a low cost. A 3-D idea can be found in a novelty shop or bookstore and purchased in volume at a reduced price. Just remember the item must be tied into your pitch. If it is useful, so much the better. The success of Al Stahl's timetable is that it provides me with a reference that I often need while reminding me of his name each time I use it.

When selecting a 3-D item for a direct mail campaign, always think of your prospects' needs, their businesses, what they do, and how they do it. Start with a list of all your business contacts, then trim the list by qualifying each prospect for the campaign using the following criteria.

1. Has the prospect used film for communications before? How? For sales promotion? For training?
2. Does your prospect have a long-term contract with one of your competitors?
3. Have you read your prospect's annual report to help you determine its readiness for film?
4. Is the prospect in a position to sponsor a film? Is the company "film wise"? Have you seen any of its past productions?
5. Do you have the correct name and title of the person responsible for the selection of film production services? The proper address? Make sure your pieces of direct mail are seen by the right people, otherwise you are wasting your time and money.

Once you have your list of qualified prospects in hand, the items and message for your 3-D campaign may be easier to pinpoint. Direct mail, like most other ventures, is not worth doing if not done well. Proper preparation and planning are the key to a successful campaign that can establish firm business contacts and the corresponding opportunities to make a sale.

STORYBOARDS AND PROMOTION

One item that filmmakers find successful as part of a direct mail campaign is a storyboard depicting their film or television spot. It is an effective means of using your current work to promote your business and generate future jobs.

A storyboard contains several picture frames, usually one for each scene in your spot or film, accompanied by appropriate captions. The front of the storyboard can also carry a sales message or mention unusual methods used in production. Where desirable, the back can be filled with additional text promoting your production facility and any special features you may offer—for example, mixing or special effects. The amount of copy is discretionary, but keep in mind that the advertising industry is built on short, to-the-point messages.

Before initiating production of a color print storyboard, obtain written permission for the use of your client's film or spot in your sales promotion efforts. Regardless of whether you have chosen as few as six frames or as many as twenty, you are still using material for which your client has paid; therefore, the client owns the rights. Take this opportunity to offer your client a quantity of the storyboards. These can be either sold to the client or presented gratis as a goodwill offering. If you approach your client to share printing expenses for the storyboards, explain the various functions they can serve: point-of-purchase (POP) displays; new product introductions; sales catalogues; dealer promotions; direct mail pieces.

When you are shooting 35mm, full color boards can be printed directly from key frames taken from one of your quality prints. Assure yourself of high quality by working from a print that has never been projected. If you are working on videotape, any number of frames can be shot directly off a good television monitor. 16mm can also be copied from a video screen, but you will get far better results by employing a still photographer on the set while you shoot in 16mm. Direct the photographer to cover the subject at or very near the motion picture camera, using the same angle and lens exposure so the resulting shots have the appearance of the subject as shown on film. For animated spots, storyboards are best produced from 35mm stills of key frames taken directly from the cels.

When selecting the frames to be used, keep the audio in mind. If you can fit matching audio under each frame (which I recommend) and have space enough for one frame for each scene in the spot, you have planned well. Generally, the amount of audio to be used as copy plus the number of scene changes determines the number of frames in your storyboard.

When you are ready to produce your printed storyboard, select a printing house experienced in this type of work. Not only is the average printer not equipped for such specialized work, he is also likely to charge more than specialty houses. Visual Promotions, Inc., one of the largest and best known printers of these colorful merchandising aids, even offers a kit of instructions for the correct preparation of the board that will help save additional cash. Generally, the printing house will need a rough layout, typed copy, and strips of 35mm film. Discuss the job with your printer in advance to insure that you have supplied everything that is needed for the job.

Once you have the boards, do not limit their use to direct mail campaigns. Carry them on sales calls; frame them and hang them on your waiting room and office walls; hand them out after screening a sample reel. The storyboard style is flash. It looks slick and tells the story in pictures. Since your audience is composed of clients or prospects looking for a visually sophisticated studio, storyboards provide an excellent spotlight on your talents as a visual communicator.

YOUR OWN PUBLIC RELATIONS

There are several options other than storyboards that provide equal opportunity to boost simultaneously your own business and that of your client. Such methods are public relations just as surely as those discussed in chapter 4, only here the emphasis is broadened to include media outside film and video, particularly print.

Whenever a production involves a product or service that is newsworthy, it is advantageous for both producer and client to exploit their work. In most cases, if there is a news angle, it is worth publishing. The type of news angle will dictate where it is published. For example, if the film covers a new product that will affect everyday life—such as the first demonstration of a videodisc—the news angle suits the mass consumer media. Information of interest to manufacturers only, on the other hand, would be better targeted at trade publications, such as *Women's Wear Daily* or *Steel World.*

Remember, nothing angers editors more than receiving a news release that has no news value and is an obvious plug. Most are willing to read news releases from recognizable sources, particularly those known to have integrity. The trick is maintaining enough objectivity about your own work to judge its value to the public. Training films, for example, are not ordinarily considered worthy of exploiting in any medium unless there is a news angle. What kind of news angle? Well, does the film utilize a new form of training methodology? Are the trainers newsmakers? Is the filmmaker a newsmaker? If Steven Spielberg made a training film, it would certainly be considered news.

Many magazines have editorial guidelines, and it is wise to write to the editor for these before sending off news releases of feature articles. Once you have become acquainted with the editorial policy, formats, and slant, you can feel confident that features written for specific client objectives will conform. Also answer the following questions for yourself before attempting to write any release or story.

1. What are the publications in this market?
2. How much space are they likely to give this story?
3. What is their level of information regarding this product or service?
4. What types of "newspeg" have the greatest appeal in this market?
5. How much rewriting or release reading time are they willing to invest in this subject?
6. What type of information is generally acceptable in this market?

Following such a review, you should be able to determine whether a release or feature story will best serve your purpose. For a feature, query the magazine about their interest: send off a one-page description of the story accompanied by suitable illustrations. Include a self-addressed, stamped envelope for return if the editor is uninterested. If you receive a go-ahead, it will most likely specify the article length in words, photo sizes, and instructions on specialized interview formats. Follow the editor's instructions for manuscript submission; otherwise, submit cleanly typed copy, double-spaced with 1½-inch margins all around.

If you decide that a feature article is needed and you are not a writer, do not hesitate to hire one. Public relations for yourself and your client are important to your success, so it is worth it to invest in professional help. If you enjoy writing, you may wish to move beyond writing for clients and submit technical articles to film trade journals.

The other written form you will utilize frequently is the news or press release. In this format, you will provide extensive information in the most concise manner. Generally, a press release touting a new product or service would include the following features: an announcement of the product's development in a summary sentence; a definition of the product and its significance; an explanation of how it works and its applications; additional product features; advantages for the consumer; documentation of claims; specifications; availability; client puff. The sample release that follows, which was prepared for a construction trade magazine, contains most of these components. Can you identify them?

VIBRO DRIVER TRIMS JOB SCHEDULE
FOR STEEL PLANT SETTLING BASINS

A vibratory driver/extractor drove pile sheets in three to four minutes per pair during construction of a new waste handling system for U.S. Steel Corporation's National Works, McKeesport, Pennsylvania. Speed of the vibratory unit cut pile driving time and costs, and permitted the job to be completed ahead of schedule, according to the contractor, Dravo Corporation.

Dravo used a Model 2-50 Vibro Driver-Extractor, purchased from L. B. Foster Company, to drive pairs of MZ27 and MZ38 steel sheet piles. The piles form sidewalls for three settling basins at National Works. Driving rate was 121 feet per hour at the start and 230 feet per hour at completion, averaging 171 feet per hour for the job.

Pile sheets were driven to refusal through Monongahela River silt and clay. The Vibro required no downtime. The only maintenance required was lubrication between shifts.

Dravo used two steam hammers—a 9B-3 and a 10B-3—to tack wall sections of piling before driving. Actual driving time for the Vibro was three to four minutes for a pair of sheets. There was no deformation from driving. The piling was cropped one foot from the top and capped with a 15-inch channel section.

The heavier sheet piling was used on the outside walls of the basins to withstand buffeting forces of the river. Because of barge activity, the outside wall of the second basin was reinforced with pile clusters. Prefabricated waler sets were barged to the job site from Dravo's Neville Island plant downriver. They were used as templates during pile driving.

The inside frameworks of the basins consisted of H-beam walers supported with horizontal pipe bracing filled with concrete. Wingwalls were added to the upstream end of each basin for protection against flotsam.

The settling basins will contain industrial wastes from the pipe, bloom, and bar mill areas at National Works. Mill scale will be collected in each basin where it will settle for periodic removal. Oil will be skimmed at the top while the remaining clean water is returned to the river. U.S. Steel's central engineering department designed the new waste handling system.

Note that client puffs must be light and woven into the story. The reader does not want to confront an advertisement in the guise of a press release, and editors are severe when confronted with too much hype.

In addition to writing releases, there is also a role for photography in public relations. Quite often a magazine will publish a picture that says quite a lot without hanging a story on it. Consider a photograph of a commercial being filmed on the Avenue of the Americas in New York City with Jack Lemmon as narrator. He wears the uniform of a Minuteman; a crowd of smiling people stands behind him. Little needs to be said except to identify the scene in a caption. Readers read pictures, as every photographer knows. We call this visual literacy.

Most of the time, however, photographs are used to illustrate a story. They help create lively layouts in otherwise stiff trade magazines. They also complement the story often by clarifying or amplifying what the writer is trying to say.

Whenever you provide a photograph for publication, be certain you have a signed model release for each person portrayed. A release should be obtained whenever you are shooting a film; you can never predict how you will publicize your work or when a performer will seek to assert individual rights or protect privacy. Legal model release forms are available from film equipment suppliers and should be used on every production. A sample follows:

MODEL AND PERFORMER'S RELEASE

Subject _____

Project #_____ Hrs. _____

For value received and without further consideration, I hereby consent that all photographs taken of me and/or recordings made of my voice and/or written extractions, in whole or in part, of such recording or musical performance at _____

on _____ 19 ___by _____

for (Company) may be used by (Company) and/or others with its consent, for the purposes of illustration, advertising, or publication in any manner.

SUBJECT _____
                        (signature)

Street _____

City _____State _____Zip _____

IF SUBJECT IS A MINOR UNDER LAWS OF STATE WHERE MODELING IS PERFORMED:

GUARDIAN _____
                        (signature)

Street _____

City _____State _____Zip _____

Note that a parental signature must be secured if you are using models who are legally under age.

Whether you use direct mail, storyboards, photographs, or feature stories, you cannot succeed unless you become promotion conscious. As you work on a day-to-day basis, stay alert to all promotional possibilities. For public relations think in terms of news angle for any kind of exploitation, exposure, or information that you can pass on to the public in a way beneficial to you and your company. At the same time, remember that any public relations must have validity in the medium you are approaching. A newspaper is usually interested in fast-breaking news stories. Most magazines lack the urgency of dailies but require stories that interest their readers. Television demands flash-type news before it provides coverage, although the proliferating television magazine programs offer new possibilities for film public relations. The key is to be alert to the opening and always be prepared.

7/HITTING THE BIG-TIME: FEATURE FILMS AND TELEVISION

What I am about to tell you was said in a private conversation, but it illustrates a prevalent attitude in Hollywood. The actor was tall and impressively built for a man in his late sixties, muscular and bearded. He had begun his career in the late 1940s and was—for one brief period—considered a major star. For all these decades, he has had a love-hate relationship with Hollywood.

"Hollywood is a materialistic jungle where the strong of

hubris, not the strong of heart or spirit, or even the intelligent, but the strong of hubris," he emphasized with clenched fist, "prey upon the weak-willed and the naive. You cannot trust anyone, not even your best friends, for they more than likely have a profit motive for being your friends. They seek you for your connections. Your agent you trust least because as he hawks your flesh, he will sell you out if there is enough profit. He will keep you from good works if he feels they are not profitable enough nor promising enough. When you're not hot, he will forget you exist."

"The studios are tiny fiefdoms run by malevolent little Napoleons who only understand the sound of an adding machine. If you print out in black and net out, they speak your language. If not, they pass you by like horse manure on the grand highway." The actor droned on and on until he ran out of energy and his voice trailed off.

He poured me a cup of hot coffee. Sitting back, a question occurred to me so I asked, "Suppose you got a call from Hollywood right now." Without blinking, he answered, "I'd be on the next plane as soon as I could pack."

Sooner or later—and probably sooner—most filmmakers dream of going Hollywood: producing a film that will enjoy wide distribution and critical acclaim. You may be making a handsome living churning out local televison spots, training films, or public service shorts, but deep in your soul you dream of larger audiences and princely earnings. You want to make it in feature films or television.

Can an independent really succeed in these fields? The answer is a qualified yes. Independents venturing into television or feature film production must have not only a firm command of all the basics, but also fortitude to withstand all the obstacles the system puts in their way. The greater riches to be earned are matched by the greater number of risks to be taken and compromises to be made on the road to success. This chapter will provide some practical methods for proceeding in these larger enterprises and suggest ways to avoid the pitfalls inherent in such ventures.

THE EXPLOITATION FILM

Hollywood today is everywhere. If you want to make a picture and can raise local capital to finance your project, then your hometown can become your Hollywood. George Romero made his classic *Night of the Living Dead* in Pittsburgh with an estimated budget of $100,000 and a local cast that was paid only after the film made a profit. To date, it has grossed $55 million.

So you can make your feature film anywhere, but what kind of film should you make? Although there are many genres from which to choose, the single formula that has proved repeatedly successful is the exploitation film. An exploitation film (explo, for short) is a low-budget feature produced for a very specific market. Gangster films, car chase films, horror films, and of course, pornographic films all fall into this classification. Such films exploit current social mores. They try to ride the crest of a wave. Each film is produced with a target audience in mind. *Super Fly* and the various *Shaft* films that followed on the heels of the black power movement are examples of the explo at its worst/best.

Let us focus on the various stages of production encountered during the making of an exploitation film and suggest possible solutions to some of the problems that can be anticipated.

The Script

Obtain a sound exploitation property. When you select a script for your film, look for a screenplay with a well-defined, suspenseful plot and some subplot structure. The story must not only keep moving, but also allow for some character development and corresponding audience identification with the characters. A human story is best: man versus man; man versus nature; man versus beast; man versus self. A film exploring the conflict between man and society usually requires more depth of meaning than an explo can handle, so avoid such themes. Remember: The exploitation film is visceral, not cerebral.

How do you find a great property? You can check with agents listed by the Writers Guild of America to find a suitable script, or you can advertise in a writer's magazine or film trade publication. The first course can cost you dearly, but the second might result in a flood of awful scripts. Protect yourself from the latter by asking initially for just a synopsis; if you are intrigued you can always request a treatment or shooting script. If you are interested in developing your own idea, consult the Writer's Guild for a list of experienced scriptwriters or talk to someone who teaches screenwriting about writing a screenplay for you.

Do not trust only your own instincts when selecting a script. After narrowing the choice to two or three, have the scripts read by several people who know how to evaluate a good story. Do not move toward production until you have found a script that excites both you and a handful of readers.

Financing

Budget your film and raise the money. After finding the right script, prepare the most skeletal budget possible, then add 25 percent for advertising, promotion, and exhibition. Prepare a written presentation for your potential investors, including a story synopsis, the script, a comprehensive budget, and a projection of estimated income from various markets: first-run theaters, drive-ins, network and independent television, cable, video, and overseas sales. The presentation should also include the limited partnership agreement under which you and your investors will operate. You will need the guidance of an attorney well-versed in investment arrangements and partnership contracts. Adhere strictly to your attorney's advice.

Locating investors is not easy. Your best bets are venture capital firms recommended by someone in the financial community. Explain your needs to the broker and follow through on all leads. Young, vigorous investment consultants often have among their clients several investors looking for unconventional projects in which to put their money. Professionals and businesspeople with solid portfolios frequently set aside a bit of gambling money, and a film that can provide them with a year's conversation may be a very attractive investment. Your partners are out there—you just have to dig a bit. Also keep in mind that when you are pitching interested investors, your track record in any aspect of film production—television spots, industrials, or educational films—should be used to boost your prospects' confidence in you and the viability of the project.

Confront the Inevitable

Earmark 25 percent of the money you raise to use for advertising and exhibition. Forget about existing distributors right from the start. Sure, you can screen your epic for them, but do not hold your breath until they sign you up. Embassy Pictures, which is one of the smallest distributors, screens between fifteen and twenty pictures per month, yet releases only about ten each year. The larger distributors reject many more per release.

Using the money set aside, you can handle your own distribution. Rent a theater for screenings following a saturation campaign on local television that uses hard-hitting spots aired during programs watched by your targeted audience. If you do very well in a test market like Cleveland or Houston, you might then generate some interest from one of the major distributors. If not, you still have acquired enough distribution experience to continue on alone.

Production

Keep production costs to a minimum by careful planning and budgeting. Borrow props and locations wherever practical. Plan to shoot as much available light as possible; you may want to consider this when choosing a script. Keep the budget for catering, costumes, and transportation spartan. Trim your budget cautiously, however, because a crew and cast that have not had a good night's sleep or a good meal will not perform at top efficiency.

Offer deferred contracts to all nonskilled labor, production assistants, and the like. Many film students eager for experience on a real shoot will gladly provide their services for the promise of payment after the film realizes a profit. Do not attempt to save money when hiring a production manager. This position must be filled by a professional, preferably with experience on the west coast or in New York. Hire your production manager early in production and listen to all his suggestions regarding the crew. A professional will know how to save you money. Do not underestimate the importance of your production manager; this individual can make you or break you. The same is true of the director of photography: Be sure to use someone experienced in handling camera and lighting crews.

Forget about name actors. Did you recognize the names of most of the stars of *Rocky* or *Star Wars* when you first saw those films? Of course not. Those successes relied on the story or production techniques, so spend your money on them instead of talent.

Convince your entire cast to work salary deferred, even if you have to promise the leads some shares in the picture's profits. Most local talent will be happy to accept this arrangement in return for the exposure. Be prepared to pay living expenses during the shoot. Attempt to hire talent with at least some on-camera experience. Stage actors who have never performed before a camera will have to learn a whole new set of techniques at your expense, so be careful in your casting.

If you have the chance to cast an "over-the-hill" Hollywood actor, by all means do so. Such performers add depth to your cast, and their experience can be invaluable to you. Who knows, you may even provide the start of a second career.

Low budget production in 35mm can be accomplished easily, but try to keep your shooting ratio down to three to one. Additional money can be saved by shooting in 16mm now that labs can acceptably blow up carefully exposed negatives. This option can save you tens of thousands of dollars but could cost you later because the major distributors will rarely screen 16mm films, even in blow-up. Although you are prepared to handle your own distribution, why throw away the chance of a major release for such a small amount relative to the entire budget? It is better to plan carefully and shoot 35mm.

If you are doing your own distribution, you might delay making the final cut until after you have shown your interlock to some small test audiences. Provide preview cards for recording reactions. A screening at a film school should be easy to arrange and can net you useful suggestions. Only after such previews should you make your final cut, basing it upon preview comments and your own good sense.

Distribution

Your advertising spots will be the key to marketing the film if you self-distribute, so take care that they are produced well. Make the spots yourself if you have background in the field; otherwise, get help from an experienced spot producer/director.

Book your spots to run during non–prime time movies. Air time is usually cheaper then, and besides, you want to grab a movie-watching audience. Whenever practical, sell your film during the broadcast of films with an appeal similar to yours.

To start, you will want to book your film for a one-week run. Shop around for a theater you can afford in a desirable location, if possible, and rent it. Then air your television spots for two weeks: one week before and one week during the run. This formula sounds rather simple, but it works. Do not, however, depend solely on your television spots. Send out press passes for everyone at the local newspaper and television and radio stations. Also provide passes for anyone who might be able to help you move the film, such as other theater owners.

Finally, take the time to compile a press book containing any reviews or feature articles about your opus. This is advance preparation in the event you decide to offer the film to a distributor. In that case you may also want to show a distributor your account books, especially if the film has made some money. Success at the box office is the primary concern of distributors.

If you are truly interested in feature films, take time to read Gregory Goodell's *Independent Feature Film Production* (see Bibliography) which provides exhaustive information on the business. I recommend especially the section on distribution and marketing, which describes the realistic, if somewhat bleak, conditions confronted by independents in these areas. If you remain undiscouraged after reading, you are indeed ready to enter the exploitation film world.

Another resource for those interested in making feature films is the Independent Feature Project (see resource list). This organization is devoted to helping independents succeed, and you will need all the help you can get.

Above all, remember that you are making a commercial film for the sole purpose of making money. The more you make, the better your position. Forget about Hollywood and Oscars, rave reviews from Rex Reed, and invitations to codirect Ingmar Bergman's next film. Forget about messages, social comments, taste, and discernment. They will have to be sacrificed. The only thing that counts in the explo game is money, money, and more money.

I call the elements that go into the making of any film venture the four Ps: property, planning, production, and promotion. Those who are optimists can also add a fifth P: prosperity.

TELEVISION BROADCAST ADVERTISING

The production of television advertising is another way of achieving wide visibility for your work, as well as excellent remuneration. While the creative end of this field is dominated by the advertising agencies, few have production facilities and thus look to independents to make their spots. There is a lot of money to be made here, but there is also a lot of competition. The broadcast advertising scene is idiosyncratic and not always ethical, so independents interested in this genre had better have their eyes wide open from the very beginning. Since the actual process of landing job contracts in this field follows the same basic pattern described throughout

this book, we will concentrate instead on some of the pecu-
liarities and moral issues confronted by the newcomer.

The Creative Process:
What Happens Before You Are Hired

With very few exceptions, a filmmaker producing spots for
advertising agencies should give up any thoughts of creative
control because that area is the sole prerogative of the agency
producer who hires you. You will not always like the shooting
script or marketing concept you are being asked to film; just
remember that your only job is to shoot the spot as directed.
You should, however, have some idea of how the creative
decisions are made.

An advertising spot is born when a client—usually an advertising manager of a corporation—decides with the agency account executive that television exposure or a new television
campaign will boost sales. The account people return to the
agency and call a production meeting to be attended by the
copywriter, art director, creative director, agency producer,
and media planner. If the client has suggested a marketing
concept, the creative team prepares a script and artwork appropriate to that concept. Otherwise, the creative team meets
separately to devise a concept for presentation to the client
and the production team.

Quite often in the advertising industry the concept is an art
director's whim influenced only by some current trend. Pursuing trends for their own sake is a disservice to both the
client and the producer. Generally, whenever one agency cop-
ies a somewhat unusual concept pioneered by a competitor,
several other agencies are pursuing the same idea. Not only is
such imitation costly, but it also proves ineffective as the air-
waves are soon blanketed with a flurry of ads, all of which
look the same.

The best concepts for television spots are simple and pure. They should be unencumbered by superfluous script or production techniques and free of any influences other than the desire to sell the advertiser's goods or services. Analyze some memorable spots you can recall. In most cases, you will discover a simple underlying concept.

Once the concept is approved, a production budget is devised. At this point the agency producer will be looking for an independent production house to film the spot. Sometimes the producer will ask for bids on a project, whereas in other instances he will select a filmmaker known to have expertise in a special field, such as cel or computer animation. Your business skills and past experience may help you land a contract at this stage, but you must also be aware of your competition and certain agency prejudices.

Realities of the Advertising World

The newcomer trying to break into the advertising game may be surprised to discover that not all hiring is done on the basis of creative merit or low bids. Although they are not universal, the problems discussed below are widespread and can be discouraging to the independent who is not prepared for them.

Perhaps the most prevalent prejudice controlling hiring—and in fact all creative aspects in broadcast advertising—is what I call "the press of vanity." Success depends on who you know. More first jobs are obtained through connections than by virtue of talent. Once you have worked in the field, future jobs depend on your most recent jobs and how they mesh with industry trends. Clios won for spots made five years ago do not necessarily guarantee a job today. You must be current and hot.

The second obstacle often confronted by independents is

what I refer to as the hardware game. Consider the careers of these two independent filmmakers: Richard is an award-winning producer. He is a creative man who keeps overhead low by renting rather then buying state-of-the-art equipment and by using top craftsmen for each spot he produces. His competitor, Paul, has two rooms full of hardware that amount to only the basics, but it is all name equipment. He also has a pretty receptionist, a coffee pot, and a soft couch. He does all the work himself, and his spots are generally second-rate. Yet it is Paul who grabs the larger number of accounts because clients are terribly impressed by his hardware. You must not become too discouraged by this scenario; Richard does get some contracts. Although he may miss out on some of the monetary rewards of the field, he maintains the integrity of his craft.

Moral Issues

The novice independent working in broadcast advertising must also be prepared to fend off assaults on his personal integrity. In many large cities the practice of giving kickbacks is prevalent, yet it is seldom discussed. It is so pervasive that few employees in the industry are left untouched and many become so sick of the practice they lose interest in their work and drop out. Unfortunately, the inexperienced can become involved almost without knowing it.

In a typical arrangement, a supplier—in this case, an independent filmmaker—tells the agency producer that the job will cost $5000. The producer then arranges for a purchase order in the amount of $5500. The extra $500 is obviously to be returned to the producer under the table. The filmmaker has participated in a crime; the producer is a thief. Those who fail to play this game are usually denied future contracts.

If you are just starting out, beware of illegal or unethical practices. At the end of your career you want to have your self-esteem intact. Do not despair of making a living in broadcast advertising while maintaining your artistic and personal integrity. There is a place for you among others who share your values and appreciate your creativity. You just have to be willing to work a bit harder to find them.

CABLE TELEVISION

Although cable televison (CTV) is not yet a stable marketplace for independent filmmakers, it certainly represents the fastest growing area in the visual communications field. Each year millions of dollars are being spent to initiate new channels, most of which are transmitted by communication satellites. The financial risk, however, is great. CBS, for example, recently failed in its attempt to offer a channel of cultural programs, although ARTS, the Hearst-ABC cultural channel, has survived. The cable market is growing in numbers and expanding in scope. More homes every year are wired for cable or have satellite dishes installed on their roofs. Such market saturation encourages fragmentation of the audiences as programming is produced for many levels of discernment and taste. That translates into greater opportunity for independents.

Let us consider the major categories of programming currently available on cable. Each of them offers some opportunity for the hustling filmmaker.

Cultural

Although presently unstable, the audience for opera, ballet, symphony music, and dramatic performances will always exist. Currently, this need is being filled on cable by Alpha Repertory Television Service (ARTS), but the Public Broadcasting Service (PBS) is also planning such a service. So far, the problem in this field has been high production costs and low advertising revenues.

News

Cable News Network (CNN), Ted Turner's big gamble, seems to have paid off and has allowed him to buy out the competing Satellite News Service (SNS). CNN often uses free-lancers and stringers for feature stories and is constantly on the lookout for newsworthy tidbits on tape or film.

Music

Music Television (MTV) features filmed presentations of rock music with stereo sound. Originally created to promote records, these films, now referred to as rock videos, have become a lucrative business of their own. Perhaps a promising band in your town needs a video for their stab at the big-time.

Adult

A number of these services, led by the Playboy Channel, now appear on cable television. Generally softcore when introduced, they gradually evolved into "clean" hardcore—that is, nudity and intercourse with little or no homosexuality or kinkiness. If you are interested in this kind of programming, there may be work for you here.

Service

Service programming is the real growth area in cable television. Health programs, twenty-four-hour weather forecasts, video games, stock market reports, and informational programming are all aspects of this category. Service channels are also being used as merchandising tools: "The Sharper Image," a show demonstrating electronic gadgets, is now airing a taped catalogue of electronic and other expensive personal products, including microtelevision sets, radios, and exercise equipment. An enterprising friend of mine now films homes and property for realtors and presents them on cable. Independents should be able to make similar inroads in this field by using some imagination.

Ethnic and Religious

Both of these classifications have great mass appeal, although offering little opportunity for independents. CBN, the Christian Broadcasting Network, is a successful enterprise presenting programming based on the concept of the American family circa 1948 and why it should survive. National Jewish Television is also off to a strong start. Several foreign language systems exist, including the major Spanish outlet, Galavision, which offers programming from Mexico, Spain, and South America, as well as original productions.

The Independent's Role

The scope of cable television is so broad that the independent must actually choose a field in which to concentrate. Once you have chosen a category and developed a possible film subject, contact the acquisition director of the appropriate cable service or services and find out how the service acquires programming. Stress the financial details. You will probably discover that at present few services have money to sink into production. Programming is generally acquired from the major studios. Therefore, if you are determined to produce for cable television, you must form your own production company and seek funding from investment sources. You can find a market for your work if the quality is good and you have done your homework.

Another area open to independents requires much less risk-taking. Almost all cable systems are in the market for shorts or intermission fillers. Such films can run anywhere from one to thirty minutes, with ten minutes the preferred length. Favorite subjects for shorts include comedy, animation, Hollywood star interviews, sports, and seasonal subjects. When filming a short be sure to capture the viewer's attention within the first minute. Also keep pacing and production values at broadcast television level. Forget about experimental films unless they are unusually clever and capture the public imagination. The acquisition director can provide valuable advice as to the most salable topics.

The exploitation film, broadcast advertising, and cable television all offer the independent the possibility of mass audiences and occasional acclaim. As we have seen, however, these fields are complicated by a seemingly endless array of problems. As a filmmaker, you must decide whether or not the obstacles one must overcome are worth the rewards. A good living can be made by those who enter these fields prepared to take the risks and work hard.

8/BIG BUSINESS: HOW THE FILMMAKER FITS IN

He wore a three-piece suit with rounded edges that appeared as if it had been pressed while he wore it. Not that it was crumpled, but Jay Gatsby would not have been caught dead in it. He was a tall man, yet his self-effacing ways made him seem of average height. Often, he would sit alone in his car and smoke a long Havana cigar via Canada and snicker to himself. My fellow creatives, other writers and directors, would nod toward him and draw circles around their temples with an index finger and mumble, "That's what eventually happens to all account men."

But Ted Westermann, a wonderful gentleman who has long since faded from the scene, was not someone you could just shrug off. He was very successful, and after some months of observation I approached him in an effort to find out why.

During a lunch break on a set I saw him laughing to himself again and decided to intrude upon his little magic world. "So what's so funny?" I asked, not waiting to be invited to sit down. Ted looked up at me and out came this loud belly laugh. "Oh, nothing . . . nothing at all," he said, still breaking up. I envied him his secret joke. We talked one hour into many hours during the passing months and became friends. I found that Ted, far from being a candidate for a fruitcake factory, was quite brilliant.

Ted was the man who called on General Motors. He did it with great skill. He constantly brought in business to our large studio, which needed a lot of business to keep going. The thought of working a large company like General Motors intimidated me. I asked Ted how he did it. "No problem," he said, "they're just people like you and me." Not satisfied, I asked, "Well, how do you keep clients eating out of your hand like you do?" Again, there was the Ted Westermann smile of confidence. "Ya gotta be funny. People have all the grief they need already. They need someone to pick them up and dust 'em off. All's you gotta do," he said, patting the ashes off the large Havana with the flamboyance of a conductor before the Bostom Symphony, "is have a good sense of humor." My God, I thought, how can a creative guy like me who is always playing a Greek tragedy have a sense of humor? "If you want to be popular anywhere . . . ya gotta have a good sense of humor," he asserted.

Ted was right. At times in my career I had to rediscover this great secret the hard way, but for the most part what he told me stuck through the years. As business flowed under the bridge, it became easier when things got tight to maintain a sense of humor. Soon I realized that no matter how big a corporation was, it was still composed of people, just as Ted said. This was the most important thing to remember when considering large accounts without the help of a wonderful Ted Westermann. He is sorely missed.

Throughout this book, we have explored the multiple and varied business opportunities available to the filmmaker willing to use some imagination and hustle. Our canvass of potential clients has included community institutions, small businesses, advertising agencies, and cable television. However, the single greatest source of jobs for independents, large corporations, has been mentioned only fleetingly. Almost every type of visual communication described can be used by some division of a large corporation. The following discussion of the filmmaker's role in big business should indicate the variety of jobs that can be gleaned from this source—if you know how to find them.

HOW TO ATTACK THE BIG CORPORATION

It was suggested in chapter 4 that an organizational chart is a useful tool when preparing to solicit business from any large corporation. Now we will take a closer look at the typical corporate structure in order to consider ways in which the filmmaker can sell his services at several levels and to several divisions within the same company.

In preparing to approach a corporation, think of yourself as a communications consultant and act accordingly. You want not only to attract business, but also to promote your services. Consider what a corporation does. It manufactures a product or prepares a service and then markets that product or service.

Although most communication will be done during the marketing phase, do not overlook the opportunities available during the production phases, perhaps in training or internal communication. Seek out the individuals in charge of each division and find out how they do their work. You may discover ways in which you as a filmmaker or audiovisual producer can help.

The chief executive officer of a corporation is usually the president and can be found at the top of every organizational chart. The filmmaker can generally bypass this office when contacting a large corporation. Concentrate instead on the officers who report directly to the president in the areas of operations or manufacturing, marketing, and finance. These operating vice presidents and their immediate assistants— managers and supervisors—are responsible for purchasing screened communication from outside vendors and are thus the proper target for the filmmaker's attention.

The corporation offers not only a wide range of business opportunities, but also the possiblity of a continuing account. To maintain such an account, your understanding of the corporate structure must go beyond the organizational framework to allow for personnel changes. During the course of a continuing account you may find that, due to personnel changes, you will be working with different executives than you started with. As a result, you may have to modify account strategy to reflect differences in the philosophies and personalities of the new people. Avoid stepping on toes by working within established channels; always present your advice and suggestions to the appropriate person. Steer clear of corporate politics. At whatever level you have access, maintain your posture as an interested and friendly observer of the corporation.

If you are a keen observer, you will be able to locate film opportunities within the corporation beyond those associated with the marketing division. Personnel departments in large organizations are quite sophisticated and eager to use modern communication methods to handle such functions as orientation, behavior modification, safety campaigns, and to introduce or review corporate policy. Video, film, or audiovisuals are also favored for training purposes; keep in mind that such jobs may be commissioned either by the personnel office or the training director of a manufacturing division. Although such films will not garner the big budgets associated with marketing, they can keep your shop busy at times when you may need new business most.

THE SPONSORED FILM

The public relations office is another source of business for the independent filmmaker. The public relations executive is responsible for communicating the corporate image to employees, the business community, and the general public. Such communications take many forms, and sometimes the chosen medium is the sponsored film.

A sponsored film is a public relations film or a public service film made by a corporation or institution to promote a positive image for itself. Although the film need not focus on a company's product or service, it will usually have a message or motive beneficial to corporate aims. Such films are presented gratis to the public. Distribution can be handled by the sponsor but is generally undertaken by a professional distributor who is paid by the sponsor for each audience screening. Each audience is also surveyed in order to give the funding company data on the film's use.

The most important aspect of making a sponsored film is determining and implementing its distribution. There is little point in obtaining budget money to produce the film unless it is backed by a good distribution plan. After all, a company that sponsors a film that never enjoys widespread screenings is unlikely to approve future film efforts. If you need help in this area, consult the two companies that currently distribute sponsored films: Modern Talking Picture Service and Association Films, Inc.

Do not forget to separate the budget for distribution from the production budget. After the film is produced, the budget for production can be laid to rest but the distribution budget may need to be carried through several fiscal years. A highly successful sponsored film may be screened for many years, thus continuing to create a positive image for the sponsor.

The sponsored film is a great opportunity for both the sponsor and the filmmaker. A company is provided with a worthwhile and beneficial project in which to invest. For the filmmaker, a well-made sponsored film can result in new sources of business as well as personal fulfillment and satisfaction. Work carefully if you get a chance to make one, and by all means read Walter Klein's excellent book on the subject, *The Sponsored Film* (see Bibliography).

THE MARKETING PROCESS

The most obvious place for the filmmaker or audiovisual producer to look for business opportunities in a corporation is the marketing division, yet even there hidden possibilities abound. Far from being limited to commercial spots and sales presentations, a role may exist for the visual communicator at almost every level of the marketing process.

Market Research

Market research is the first stage in the marketing process, especially when a new product is introduced. Researchers analyze surveys, company records, industry data, census figures, and other factors to determine the market potential of a product. Because corporate investment in further development and marketing of a product hinges on accurate market research, procedures and data are continuously verified, reviewed, and updated.

Although market research has not made use of visual communications thus far, the potential is certainly evident. By videotaping surveys, for example, it would be possible to analyze not only answers to questions, but also body language, facial expression—in fact, every visual nuance. An enterprising filmmaker, possibly teamed with a behavioral scientist, should be able to find a lucrative career in this field.

Planning

Planning, the second phase of marketing, establishes the company's mission, scope, and goals by producing a situation analysis and determining marketing objectives. A resourceful audiovisual producer can provide a visual presentation of the marketing plan to be communicated to marketing staff and corporate executives. Slide shows accompanied by a tape or oral script are preferable to film or video in this situation because they permit flexibility in the continuity of the visual presentation and readily accommodate frequent modification.

Once the market plan is completed, product planning and development (PP&D) begin. Here again the audiovisual producer can play a role in the screening and appraisal of new product ideas or actual product prototypes. Presentations can be simplified further by using closed circuit television where available. Whereas the final management review formerly rested upon a written planning and development reference guide, the videomaker or audiovisual producer can now offer a cassetted reference guide backed with figure charts.

Distribution and Pricing

In the next step of the marketing process, product distribution channels are established. Any mediamaker should be alert when distribution is mentioned. Distribution means communication, and effective communication today means some type of audiovisual. When developing a distribution network for a new product, executives consider various alternatives and then select a specific type of distribution, as well as appropriate salespeople, agents, and distributors. Once a written plan is developed, the entire concept is evaluated and, if necessary, reworked. Finally, a distribution channel reference guide is prepared. At each of these stages, the mediamaker has an opportunity to assist with corporate communication.

Once distribution has been determined, pricing is established. This is the realm of industry specialists, and no realistic role exists for the filmmaker at this stage. After pricing, however, the company will engage in advertising, public relations, and a sales campaign. These are the natural markets for the filmmaker, whose function in each phase has been discussed extensively earlier in this book.

Campaign Appraisal

After a campaign is run, its effectiveness is measured by various means including incoming letters, inquiry reports, readership studies, awareness and/or reference studies, and other market tests. Depending on the operation, a visual presentation may be appropriate. Consider inquiry handling, for example. When an inquiry is received on a new product it represents a prospective client; such leads must be communicated to the sales force promptly and handled by them efficiently. The knowledgeable filmmaker can sell the sales promotion manager a film, slide show, or tape that emphasizes the importance of correct inquiry handling. The filmmaker can also seek funding for an industrial educational film on inquiry handling and offer it to other corporations as a refresher course.

The legal aspects of marketing can also benefit from the input of a capable filmmaker. Marketing legislation, patent and trademark protection, distribution contracts, consumer, fair trade and ecology laws, must all be reviewed constantly by executives, yet many companies are unequipped to provide such information. You can help by proposing an annual slide and/or tape review, which would be researched by you or a freelance writer. Considering the increasing complexity of the marketplace and heightened consumer sensibilities, the market for such audiovisual services should continue to grow.

By now, it should be apparent that big business offers multiple opportunities for the well-prepared filmmaker or audiovisual producer who is willing to present innovative approaches to traditional problems. In this respect, the independent filmmaker relates to the large corporation in exactly the same manner as any other client. The strategy remains the same whether the end product is a television spot, sales promotion video cassette, or sponsored film. The goal is to find business and fulfill yourself as a mediamaker while serving your client's best interests.

A good living can be earned by the independent filmmaker. Financial success is currently achieved by finding and nurturing a wide variety of clients—by hustling and always producing quality work. The road for the independent may ease in the future. Videodisc and other advanced technologies may permit filmmakers not only to control the artistic content of their work but also allow them to distribute their films directly to the public, thus reaping the appropriate compensation. Until then, it is enough that filmmakers with talent, business sense, and fortitude can make money while pursuing a craft they love.

GLOSSARY

Abstract A decorative or mood-setting background that is nonrepresentational and related to no specific location.

Academy Leader A numbered strip of film on each reel of a feature that assists projectionists in synchronizing the end of one reel with the beginning of the next. The strip runs for eight seconds and was devised by the Academy of Motion Picture Arts and Sciences.

Account A client or customer of a supplier or advertising agency who purchases goods and services for advertising production.

Account Conflict A situation resulting when competing clients—for example, companies manufacturing the same product—are handled by the same supplier.

Account Executive The agency employee who maintains liaison between the advertising agency (or production company) and the client. Develops and controls the business for the company represented. Also known as contact, account representative, or account manager.

Account Supervisor Individual who supervises the work of the account executive(s).

Action 1. Movement of a subject before the camera. 2. A director's signal for such movement and the shooting of that movement.

Agent An individual who is paid to negotiate the buying or selling of goods and services without taking title to such goods or services.

Air Date A position or broadcast date for a television or radio program or commercial.

Alternative Sponsorship Occurs when two or more companies each buy a segment of time to advertise in turn—whether day by day, week by week, or program by program—within the same television or radio time slot.

Ambient Light Undirected light that provides general illumination for a scene or set.

Ambient Sound Sound reflected from interior sources rather than picked up directly from a sound source.

Angle Shot A shot continuing the action of a preceding shot, but from a different angle.

Animation The creation of the impression of movement.

Answer Print The first print of a film in release form that combines sound and picture (if a sound film). It is offered by the lab to the producer and/or director for approval prior to ordering quantity prints.

Apple Box A square riser used to raise the height of a performer or prop.

Art Director 1. In film or television, the designer and supervisor of set construction. 2.   In an advertising agency, the art director is responsible for the development of design and supervises final artwork for ads.

Baby Spotlight A small spotlight, often used on faces. Also known as dinky, inkie, inky, or inky dink.

Background The setting over which animated cels are photographed. In live-action film, background is the setting behind the action.

Background Light The light that illuminates the shot's background.

Backlight A light behind actors or objects on the set that renders increased separation from set background and gives the impression of depth.

Back Lot The portion of a major studio equipped with streets, false-front buildings, and other details that simulate location shooting.

Barndoors Opaque (usually matte black) metal sheets hinged to a frame that are placed in front of a light to permit control of the light.

Barney Lightweight, padded covering placed around a camera to insulate motor sound. Sometimes a barney is heat-wired to assist camera function during extreme cold.

Beat A predesignated pause in an actor's delivery.

Bit A single action or scene.

Blimp A covering for a camera, usually hard and shaped exactly to the camera and its fittings, used in the same manner as a barney.

Bounce Light Indirect lighting, usually reflected off walls, ceilings, or reflectors.

Broad A 2000-watt light in a boxlike lamphouse, used as a soft floodlight for illuminating wide areas.

Burn-in A photographic double exposure, usually used for titles.

Buyout A one-time payment to talent for all rights to a performance (as opposed to a residual schedule).

Camera Angle The camera's viewpoint.

Canvass A round of visits or phone calls to new or regular clients to increase sales or business.

CATV Community antenna television; a subscription service wherein individual homes are wired from a central antenna.

CCTV Closed circuit television, used for internal communication in large institutions.

Cel A transparent sheet of plastic on which a figure to be animated is painted.

Client Individual or business who employs the services of an advertising agency or production house.

Clio Award presented at the American Television and Radio Commercials Festival.

Close-up (CU) Emphasis shot that calls attention to a face, inscription on an object, or any other person or thing viewed at close range.

Color Correction Modification of tonal values with the use of tinted filters, usually done at dry-lab printer.

Color Temperature In photography, the degrees Kelvin (K) of a light source. High temperatures produce blue tones or cast, low temperatures produce red tones.

Composite A synchronization of picture and sound in a short piece of film. See also *interlock*.

Composition In photography, the relative relationships between objects and backgrounds before the camera. Also a consideration in light and shade balance.

Consumer Advertising Advertising directed at the public as a whole rather than at a specific profession or industry.

Contingencies Budget allowances for unforeseen circumstances that might delay the shoot schedule.

Continuity The progressive flow of events in the story line showing logical development of characters and plot.

Continuity Cutting Editing film or tape to present action in a smooth, logical flow that preserves the illusion of reality for the audience.

Cookie A patterned screen placed in front of a light to form interesting patterns on the set background.

Copy Writing for advertising.

Copy Chief Formerly, the agency supervisor of writing; now archaic since art and copy departments have merged.

Copywriter Individual who writes advertising or editorial copy.

CPB The Corporation for Public Broadcasting; administers federal monies allocated for public broadcasting.

Crawl Roll A drumlike mechanism on which titles and credits are placed for filming or taping.

Creative Pertaining to the process of conceiving, developing, and executing advertising ideas.

Creative Director (CD) Individual who manages agency creative personnel, such as writers and artists.

Credits Acknowledgment and identification of actors and crew members at the end of a film or video; also the title of the work at both the opening and closing of a film.

Cucalorus Spotlight screen or filter used to project a specific shape in shadow or outline a form on a backdrop. Also called cuckoo-lorus, cukaloris, cookie, and cuke.

Cue Card A large card bearing the lines to be spoken by a performer. Also called idiot card.

Cut 1. An instantaneous scene change. 2. Director's signal to stop shot and action. 3. A physical cut on film segments during the editing process.

Cyclorama A curved backdrop used to give the effect of sky or distance. Also called cyc.

Dailies Work prints made on a daily basis as the shoot continues, from which the best takes are selected. Also known as rushes.

Day for Night Daylight exterior shots that simulate night by using filters.

Depth of Field The amount of area or object photographed that is in sharp focus compared to foreground and background. The depth of field narrows as the lens aperture opens.

Direct Mail Use of the postal system to deliver advertising.

Director The individual who interprets the script and supervises its filming.

Dissolve A superimposition of two scenes—one fading in and the other fading out—varying in length for desired effect.

Documentary Presentation of actual events within a time frame.

Dolly A small wheeled platform for the camera used to shoot movement before the action.

Door Opener An inexpensive gift from a salesperson offered as an inducement to gain a prospect's attention.

Double Exposure In photography, either a superimposed shot, or two or more shots taken at different times on the same film. Also called side-by-side or vignette.

Dramatic Scene A confrontation.

Dubbing Rerecording dialogue, music, or sound effects to complete the soundtrack of a film.

Editor In video and filmmaking, the individual who cuts the film and organizes the takes to produce a final print. The cutting is done electronically in video.

Effect Technical creation of visual or auditory illusion.

Elements Package All negative film elements essential to produce a master from which prints are derived.

Emulsion Speed The photographic sensitivity of a film stock to light exposure. Usually expressed as an index number.

Envelope Stuffer A printed advertising piece enclosed with a bill or other matter in a mailing envelope.

Episodic Script or film structure giving strong emphasis to incidents while de-emphasizing continuity and the progression toward a climax. *Jeremiah Johnson* and *M*A*S*H* are episodic films.

Establishing Shot An opening shot providing a comprehensive view of a scene that in subsequent action will be shot from closer positions.

ETV Educational television; the transmission of academic instruction for home and classroom viewing.

Executive Creative Director The top person responsible for an agency's creative team.

Exploitation Film A low budget picture for a specialized audience; subjects include gothic, horror, bikers, rock, beach bikinis.

Exposition Introduction of information from the past necessary to the advancement of the plot.

Exposure Meter A device that reads the amount of light in a given location.

Exteriors (EXT) Outdoor shots.

Extreme Close-up (ECU) A very strong emphasis shot, as when a mouth fills the frame.

Extreme Long Shot (ELS) A shot that reduces the size of a subject in relation to its background to a greater degree than a long shot.

Fade A gradual obliteration of an image by means of steadily closing down the camera aperture.

Feathered Light The creation of shading or falloff by using only the weaker edge of a light.

Fill Light A secondary light on a set intended to prevent excessive light and shade contrast from the key light.

Film Chain A mechanical and electronic device used to convert the film and/or slides to a video signal.

Film Clip Short film footage used for insertion in program material.

Film Loop A piece of motion picture film spliced into a continuous and unending sequence.

Film Perforation The holes on film used by the sprockets of a camera or projector to advance it.

Filmstrip A motion picture film produced as a series of still photographs to be shown as such.

Fine Cut A finished work print, fully edited and ready for approval prior to negative matching and production for distribution.

Fiscal Year A period of roughly twelve months in length, designated by an organization as its basic financial planning unit.

Flier A printed piece, usually consisting of a single sheet, used for advertising as a handout or mailing piece.

Flip Chart A card bearing one of a sequence of messages for use in a presentation.

Floodlamp A light that illuminates a wide area. Also called flood or scoop.

Focus The degree of clarity seen through lens or projected image.

Follow Focus Focus setting change to keep a specific object in sharp focus as scene is shot.

Frame 1. Individual picture on film or videotape. 2. To compose a shot.

Full Shot A shot that takes in all of a subject.

Gaffer An electrical assistant on a production.

Gobbo An opaque screen for cutting down unwanted light from the camera lens. Also gobo.

Golden Time Time for which workers are compensated at special overtime rates, as indicated by union contracts.

Graininess On film emulsion, the size and separation of the individual silver halide particles. Very sensitive emulsions are usually grainy.

Grip A general handyman on a production.

Half Apple A stand for performers or props lower than an apple box.

Hook A striking incident, unique action, or the like, used to capture audience interest in the beginning of a picture.

Interlock The edited work print and rough soundtrack set up in synchronous parallel for approval presentation.

Jump Cut A cut that appears abrupt or out of continuity because some element of the action has been omitted, particularly in a shot from the same angle.

Key Light The primary light source in a shot.

Kicker A rim light used to define the outline of a subject, to separate the subject from the background. Also called edge light, skimmer, and separation light.

Leave Behind A document left with a prospect by a salesman at the conclusion of a sales call.

Lip Synchronization (Lip Sync) The coincidence of lip movement and sounds of speech as normally seen and heard.

Long Shot (LS) A shot that relates the subject to the background, often used as an orientation or establishing shot.

Marketing The process of product or service development, pricing, packaging, advertising, merchandising, sales, and distribution.

Marketing Director The individual responsible for the review and approval of marketing plans, sometimes including sales management.

Marketing Plan The strategy for marketing a product or service.

Market Research Research necessary to supply data for effective marketing of consumer goods and services.

Master Shot The long shot in which all action in a scene takes place. The same action is repeated for the medium shot (MS) and close-up (CU) that are usually cut into the scene.

Medium Close-up (MCU) The shot between a medium and a close-up.

Medium Long Shot (MLS) The shot between a medium and long shot.

Medium Shot (MS) A shot of the subject with only incidental background.

Merchandising In the sales promotion process, making goods or services attractive and conspicuous.

MOS "Mit out sound," an abbreviated term meaning silent filming, originated by an old German director with a heavy accent.

Narration Voice-over commentary that is spoken off screen by a voice that may or may not be identified.

Optical Effects Optical or electronic manipulation of a motion picture scene. Methods include wipes, dissolves, and fades.

Pan A horizontal camera movement to make a panoramic shot.

PBS Public Broadcasting Service; a television system sponsored by contributions and public funds such as taxes.

Pencil Test The filmed rough sketches in an animation sequence prepared prior to cleanup and transfer to cels.

Per Diem A daily cost allowance or fee for travel expenses or services.

Picture-line Standard The standard number of scan lines (horizontal electronic scanning lines) on a television screen. In the United States, 525 lines are the standard.

Piggyback Two unrelated commercials by the same sponsor aired back-to-back, usually paired for purchase as a single unit.

Plot A writer's dramatized plan of action for manipulating audience emotions.

Plot Line The story line. Also, the line of dialogue essential to the development and/or understanding of the plot.

Post Synchronization Soundtrack recording after the picture is completed. Many European films are shot without sound and post synched in various languages for distribution.

Presynchronization Recording the soundtrack before filming. This is usually done on animated films.

Process Shot A shot in which the foreground action is staged against a backscreen projection of stills or motion picture footage.

Propaganda Communications intended to influence belief and action.

Proposal Outline A brief statement of purpose, target audience, concept, and specifications for a proposed screened communication production.

Protagonist A film's central character in whose fate the audience will be most interested and with whom the audience will most identify.

Publicity Information regarding a person, corporation, or product, released for free use by the media.

Public Relations Activities of persons or organizations intended to promote good will toward themselves or their goods and services.

Public Service Advertising Advertising carried by the media without charge to propagate socially important information and promote good will.

Raw Stock Unexposed motion picture film.

Release A legal contract assigning a person's rights to the use of his name, likeness, ideas, or property to another party in return for a stated consideration.

Release Print The final print run for distribution after all corrections are done from the answer print.

Residual A royalty paid to a performer or other person by a television or radio station or advertiser for each broadcast of a program or commercial. Rates are usually established by union contract.

Reversal Film Film that is processed to produce a positive image instead of a negative. This process is generally used when the clarity of the first generation print is important.

Rough Cut An assembly of all the takes to be used in the work print without fine cutting or trimming and marked effect for transitions. The rough cut is always in sequence per script.

Rushes *See dailies.*

Scene One continuous segment of action in a film.

Scrim A fine, translucent cloth or screen used to diffuse light as a backdrop or over a light.

Segue Smooth transition from one sound to another, particularly in a musical presentation, as from one musical number to another in a medley.

Sequence A series of shots comprising a brief continuity within a film to dramatize a unified thought or theme.

Shot A single run of the camera or the results on film of such a run.

Slide Commercial A television commercial with a video sequence made up wholly, or in part, of slides rather than film.

Sound Effects Track The magnetic track that contains the sound effects other than dialogue or music.

Soundtrack Any magnetic or optical sound recording, whether separate or a mixed composite of music, dialogue, and effects.

Special Effects Multiple image, split screen, miniature, or any unusual effect not obtainable without extra manipulative effort.

Storyboard A presentation panel of illustration of the various shots proposed or planned for a television commercial, animated program, or motion picture, with notes regarding filming, audio components, and script arranged in consecutive order.

Story Line A screenplay's plot development.

Story Treatment A semidramatized, present tense, preliminary structuring of a screenplay.

Subplot A story within a story, generally involving subordinate characters and developed in terms of action parallel to that of the main plot. Its purpose is to provide relief from the main plot tension and add interest to the production.

Suspense Uncertainty of outcome; the fear that something will or will not happen.

Swish Pan A transitional device in which a pan is so fast that the images blur; often used to change scenes.

Synopsis A brief outline of a proposed film's content.

Take Film or tape of a single shot.

Talent Actors, musicians, and other performers.

Target Audience The audience intended to be reached by an advertiser in using a given communications medium or set of media.

Teaser Intriguing pretitle action used to capture audience attention, especially in a television movie.

Title The name of a film or any information inscription on the film.

Trade Name A name applied to a type of goods or service furnished by a company that may also have the exclusive character of a trademark. Also the name under which a company or person does business. Xerox, for example, is both a trademark and a trade name.

Trade Paper or Magazine A periodical edited for the interest of persons associated with a specific trade or industry.

Trade Show A special temporary exhibit of goods or services for trade buyers, often done in collaboration with other exhibitors. Also called a trade convention.

Transition The smooth passage from one episodic part to another, maintaining audience orientation and the established mood of the film.

Trucking Moving the camera by using a dolly in order to follow the general movement of the subject.

Waist Shot A shot of a person from the waist up.

Walk-through An early rehearsal to work out wrinkles for both the performers and the crew. Also called a dry run.

Wild Shot A shot with no synchronous sound relationship, such as an establishing shot or a shot used for transition only.

Wild Spot A spot commercial announcement for a national or regional advertiser used on local station breaks. Also called spot announcement.

Wipe An optical transition on film in which a second scene seems to be replacing a first scene in a progressive revelation.

Work Print A film print used for final editing to produce the answer print by matching the cuts with the original negative after the work print editing is completed.

Zoom Lens A lens with a variable focal length for simulating a camera moving into or out of the scene.

SELECTED
BIBLIOGRAPHY

BOOKS ON FILMMAKING

The Filmmaking Process

Bobker, Lee R. *Making Movies from Script to Screen*. New York: Harcourt Brace Jovanovich, 1973.

Book, Albert C., and Norman D. Cary. *The Radio and Television Commercial*. Chicago: Crain Books, 1978.

Canemaker, John. *The Animated Raggedy Ann & Andy*. New York: Bobbs-Merrill, 1977.

Courter, Philip. *The Filmmaker's Craft*. New York: Van Nostrand Reinhold, 1982.

London, Mel. *Getting into Film*. New York: Ballantine Books/ Random House, 1977.

Malkiewicz, J. Kris. *Cinematography.* New York: Van Nostrand Reinhold, 1973.

Ritsko, Alan J. *Lighting for Location Motion Pictures.* New York: Van Nostrand Reinhold, 1979.

The Business of Filmmaking

Brown, William O. *Low Budget Features.* Privately published, 1977. (P.O. Box 2641, Hollywood, CA 90028)

Chamness, Danford. *The Hollywood Guide to Film Budgeting and Script Breakdown.* Los Angeles: Stanley J. Brooks, 1981.

Farber, Donald C., and Paul A. Baumgarten. *Producing, Financing, and Distributing Film.* New York: Drama Book Specialists, 1973.

Goodell, Gregory. *Independent Feature Film Production.* New York: St. Martin's Press, 1982.

Gregory, Mollie. *Making Films Your Business.* New York: Schocken Books, 1979.

Klein, Walter J. *The Sponsored Film.* New York: Hastings House, 1976.

Leedy, David J. *Motion Picture Distribution.* Privately published, 1980. (P.O. Box 27845, Los Angeles, CA 90027)

Mayer, Michael F. *The Film Industries: Practical Business/Legal Problems in Production, Distribution, and Exhibition.* New York: Hastings House, 1973.

Wiese, Michael. *The Independent Filmmaker's Guide: How to Finance, Produce, and Distribute Your Short and Documentary Films.* Sausalito, CA: M. Wiese Film Productions, 1981.

Film History

Cabarga, Leslie. *The Fleischer Story.* Franklin Square, NY: Nostalgia Press, 1976.

Maltin, Leonard. *Of Mice and Magic.* New York: McGraw-Hill, 1980.

Scriptwriting

Edmonds, Robert. *Scriptwriting for the AudioVisual Media.* New York: Teachers College Press, 1978.

Egri, Lajos. *The Art of Dramatic Writing.* New York: Simon & Schuster, 1960.

Giustini, Rolando. *The Film-Script: A Writer's Guide.* Englewood Cliffs, NJ: Prentice-Hall, 1980.

Nash, Constance, and Virginia Oakey. *The Screenwriter's Handbook.* New York: Barnes & Noble Books/Harper & Row, 1978.

Reference Books for the Filmmaker

Bension, Shmuel, ed. *New York Production Manual, 1981: The Producer's Masterguide for Motion Picture, Television, Commercials, and Videotape Industries.* New York: New York Production Manual, 1981.

Jesuale, Nancy J., and Ralph L. Smith. *The CTIC Cablebooks.* Arlington, VA: Cable Television Information Center, 1982.

Pagano, Anne L., ed. *Cable Advertising Directory.* Washington, D.C.: National Cable Television Association, 1981.

Parlato, Sal. *Films Ex Libris.* Jefferson, NC: McFarland, 1980.

Parlato, Sal. *Films—Too Good for Words.* New York: Bowker, 1973.

Parlato, Sal. *Super Films.* Metuchen, NJ: Scarecrow Press, 1976.

Ziegler, Sherilyn K., and Herbert H. Howard. *Broadcast Advertising: A Comprehensive Working Textbook*. Columbus, OH: Grid Publishing, 1978.

READINGS FOR THE INDEPENDENT SMALL BUSINESSMAN

General Business Practice and Philosophy

Ballas, George C., and Dave Hollas. *The Making of an Entrepreneur: Keys to Your Success*. Englewood Cliffs, NJ: Prentice-Hall, 1980.

Baty, Gordon B. *Entrepreneurship: Playing to Win*. Reston, VA: Reston Publishing, 1974.

Book of Business Knowledge. New York: Boardroom Books, 1979.

Brandt, Steven C. *Entrepreneuring: The Ten Commandments for Building a Growth Company*. New York: Addison-Wesley, 1982

Carrol, Frieda. *Survival Handbook for Small Business*. Atlanta, GA: Bibliotheca Press, 1981.

Cook, Peter D. *Start and Run Your Own Successful Business: An Entrepreneur's Guide*. New York: Beaufort Books, 1982.

Deiner, Royce. *How to Finance a Growing Business*. Woodstock, NY: Beekman Publishers, 1974.

Gordon, Barbara, and Elliot Gordon. *How to Survive in the Freelance Jungle*. New York: Executive Communications, 1980.

Kirzner, Israel M. *Competition and Entrepreneurship*. Chicago: University of Chicago Press, 1978.

Linneman, Robert E. *Turn Yourself On: Goal Planning for Success*. New York: Rosen Press, 1970.

Mancuso, Joseph, ed. *The Entrepreneur's Handbook*. Dedham, MA: Artech House, 1974.

Schollhammer, Hans, and Arthur Kuriloff. *Entrepreneurship and Small Business Management*. New York: John Wiley & Sons, 1979.

Scott, William. *How to Earn More Profits through the People Who Work for You: A Practical Handbook for Managers and Small Business Owners to Hiring, Evaluating and Motivating Employees*. Englewood Cliffs, NJ: Prentice-Hall, 1982.

Stevens, Mark. *How to Run Your Own Business Successfully*. New York: Monarch Press, 1978.

Stickney, John. *Self-Made: Braving an Independent Career in a Corporate Age*. New York: Putnam, 1980.

White, Richard M. *The Entrepreneur's Manual: Business Start-Ups, Spin-Offs, and Innovative Management*. Radnor, PA: Chilton, 1976.

Advertising

Amsteil, Joel. *What You Should Know about Advertising*. Dobbs Ferry, NY: Oceana Publications, 1979.

Anuta, Larry. *The Complete Mail Sales Promotion*. Concord, CA: Surevelation, 1977.

Fletcher, Winston. *Teach Yourself Advertising*. Teach Yourself Series. New York: David McKay, 1978.

Garfunkle, Stanley. *Developing the Advertising Plan: A Practical Guide*. New York: Random House, 1980.

Hodgson, Richard S. *Direct Mail and Mail Order Handbook*. Chicago: Dartnell Corporation, 1980.

Hoke, H. *What You Should Know about Direct Mail*. Dobbs Ferry, NY: Oceana Publications, 1966.

Kleppner, Otto. *Advertising Procedure*. 8th ed. Englewood Cliffs, NJ: Prentice-Hall, 1983.

Kincaid, William M. *Promotion: Products, Services and Ideas.* Columbus, OH: Charles E. Merrill, 1981.

Kuswa, Webster. *Big Paybacks from Small Budget Advertising.* Chicago: Dartnell Corporation, 1982.

Norins, Hanley. *The Compleat Copywriter: A Comprehensive Guide to All Phases of Advertising Communication.* Melbourne, FL: R. E. Krieger, 1980.

Pokress, E. *Advertising and Public Relations.* Allenhurst, NJ: Aurea, n.d.

Smith, Cynthia, S. *How to Get Big Results from a Small Advertising Budget.* New York: Dutton, 1973.

Sutton, Cort. *Advertising Your Way to Success: How to Create Best-Selling Advertisements in All Media.* Englewood Cliffs, NJ: Prentice-Hall, 1981.

Wademan, Victor. *Money-Making Advertising: Guide to Advertising That Sells.* New York: John Wiley & Sons, 1981.

Welch, Ditt T., Jr. *Advertising First Class on Any Budget.* Mesquite, TX: Ide House, 1982.

Selling

Adelman, Conrad. *How to Manage Your Sales Time.* Hillsdale, NJ: IBMS, Inc.

Ades, Leslie J. *Increasing Your Sales Potential.* New York: Harper & Row, 1981.

Aronson, Sam. *Everyone's Guide to Opening Doors by Telephone.* San Mateo, CA: S. Aronson, 1981.

Bender, James F. *How to Sell Well: The Art and Science of Professional Salesmanship.* New York: McGraw-Hill, 1971.

Bobrow, Edwin E. *How to Sell Your Way into Your Own Business.* New York: Sales and Marketing Management Magazine, 1977.

Burstein, Milton B. *What You Should Know about Selling and Salesmanship.* Dobbs Ferry, NY: Oceana Publications, 1969.

Ellman, Edgar. *Recruiting and Selecting Profitable Sales Personnel.* New York: Van Nostrand Reinhold, 1981.

Fellows, Hugh P. *Art and Skill of Talking with People: A New Guide to Personal and Business Success.* Englewood Cliffs, NJ: Prentice-Hall, 1964.

Kinder, Jack, Jr., et al. *Winning Strategies in Selling.* Englewood Cliffs, NJ: Prentice-Hall, 1981.

Peterson, Ken T. *How to Sell Successfully by Phone.* Chicago: Dartnell Corporation, 1975.

Steinberg, Jules. *Customers Don't Bite: Selling with Confidence.* New York: Fairchild, 1970.

Public Relations

Barber, Harry L. *How to Steal a Million Dollars in Free Publicity.* Newport Beach, CA: Newport Publishing, 1982.

Benn, Alec. *The Twenty-Three Most Common Mistakes in Public Relations.* New York: American Management Association, 1982.

Bernays, Edward L. *Public Relations.* Norman, OK: University of Oklahoma Press, 1977.

Bowman, P., and N. Ellis. *A Manual of Public Relations.* New York: State Mutual Bank, 1977.

Culligan, Matthew J., and Dolph Greene. *Getting Back to the Basics in Public Relations and Publicity.* New York: Crown, 1982.

Delacorte, Toni, et al. *How to Get Free Press: A Do It Yourself Guide to Promote Your Interests, Organization, or Business.* San Francisco: Harbor, 1981.

Kadon, John, and Ann Kadon. *Successful Public Relations Techniques.* Scottsdale, AZ: Modern Schools, 1976.

Lewis, H. G. *How to Handle Your Own Public Relations.* Chicago: Nelson-Hall, 1976.

MacDougall, Curtis. *Interpretative Reporting.* New York: Macmillan, 1977.

Samstag, Nicholas. *Persuasion for Profit.* Norman, OK: University of Oklahoma Press, 1957.

Simon, Raymond, ed. *Perspectives in Public Relations.* Norman, OK: University of Oklahoma Press, 1966.

Marketing

Bradway, B. M., and M. A. Frenzel. *Strategic Marketing: A Handbook for Entrepreneurs and Managers.* Reading, MA: Addison-Wesley, 1982.

Breen, George Edward. *Do-It-Yourself Marketing Research.* New York: McGraw-Hill, 1981.

Buen, Victor P., and Carl Heyel, eds. *Handbook of Modern Marketing.* New York: McGraw-Hill, 1970.

Luther, William M. *The Marketing Plan: How to Prepare and Implement It.* New York: American Management Association, 1982.

RESOURCES FOR THE FILMMAKER

TRADE PUBLICATIONS AND PERIODICALS

Advertising Age, 740 Rush Street, Chicago, IL 60611. Published weekly, this is the oldest and largest trade magazine in advertising.

American Film, American Film Institute, The Kennedy Center for the Performing Arts, Washington, D.C. 20566. Published monthly.

American Cinematographer, 1782 North Orange Drive, Hollywood, CA 90028. Published monthly.

American Showcase, 30 Rockefeller Plaza, New York, NY 10020. Published annually to display advertising talent.

Association of Cinema & Video Laboratories, P.O. Box 34932, Bethesda, MD 20034. Annual directory provides editorial guidelines and standards.

Backstage, 330 West 42nd Street, New York, NY 10036; 5670 Wilshire Boulevard, Los Angeles, CA 90036; 841 North Addison Avenue, Elmhurst, IL 60126. Published weekly.

The Creative Black Book, Friendly Publications, Inc., 401 Park Avenue South, New York, NY 10016. Annual advertising showcase.

Hollywood Production Manual, 1322 North Cole Avenue, Hollywood, CA 90028. Annual with periodic updates. This is an invaluable guide for the filmmaker, covering current rates, facilities, budget items, and other production problems.

Hollywood Reporter, 6715 Sunset Boulevard, Hollywood, CA 90028; 1501 Broadway, New York, NY 10036. Published weekly.

Index to Kodak Information, 343 State Street, Rochester, NY 14650. Annual guide to the technical literature published by Kodak. Ask for pamphlet L-5.

Legal and Business Problems of Financing Motion Pictures, Practicing Law Institute, 810 Seventh Avenue, New York, NY 10019.

Millimeter Magazine, 826 Broadway, New York, NY 10003. Published monthly with emphasis on television spot production.

Motion Picture Almanac and *Television Almanac,* 159 West 53rd Street, New York, NY 10019. These annual publications are crammed with industry information and a who's who section listing talent and executives.

Motion Picture, TV and Theatre Directory, Tarrytown, NY 10591. A biannual directory of services.

Variety and *Daily Variety,* 154 West 46th Street, New York, NY 10036; 1400 North Cahuenga Boulevard, Hollywood, CA 90028. To order daily, use Hollywood address.

Writer's Digest Magazine, 9933 Alliance Road, Cincinnati, OH
45242. Monthly how-to magazine.
Writer's Market, 9933 Alliance Road, Cincinnati, OH 45242.
Annual reference book.

ORGANIZATIONS THAT AID FILMMAKERS

Academy Players Directory, Academy of Motion Pictures Arts
and Sciences, Wilshire Boulevard, Beverly Hills, CA 90211.
Provides casting assistance by offering photo listings of talent and corresponding information on agents.
Association Films, Inc., 866 Third Avenue, New York, NY
10022. A distributor of sponsored films.
Copyright Office, Library of Congress, Washington D.C. 20540.
Can provide information on sound recording copyright
laws.
Director's Guild of America Directory, 7950 West Sunset Bou-
levard, Los Angeles, CA 90046.
Independent Cinema Artists & Producers (ICAP), 625 Broad-
way, New York, NY 10012. Offers distribution assistance to
the independent, primarily in placing short films on televi-
sion and in other markets.
The Independent Feature Project, 80 East 11th Street, New
York, NY 10003. Helps independents distribute feature
films.
Modern Talking Picture Service, 45 Rockefeller Plaza, New
York, NY 10020. The oldest and largest sponsored film distributor.
Visual Promotions, Inc., 145 West 45th Street, New York, NY
10036. They will print your television spot storyboard for
promotional use.
Writer's Guild, West: 8955 Beverly Boulevard, Los Angeles, CA

90048. East: 22 West 48th Street, New York, NY 10036. Publishes annual directory listing writing credits and literary agents.

INDEX